LOVE IS ALWAYS THE ANSWER

OUR LIVES are an unexpected blend of many experiences, and most people live many lives within one. In *Love is Always the Answer*, Miriam Freedman begins by sharing her childhood experience of hiding for months in a basement during the Holocaust, then living in Israel during its early formation, and finally moving to London where she became a teacher of yoga and spiritual arts. There she met another, most profound teacher, a Russian woman named Mrs. Irina Tweedie, who had herself studied with a Sufi master in India. This specialized form of teaching was geared toward awakening love in one's heart. This book chronicles the spiritual relationship between these two women as they reveal their knowledge and wisdom, analyze significant dreams, and share direct experiences of altered states. An inspiration, and a trustworthy guide to those on a spiritual path.

Also by Miriam Freedman

Under the Mango Tree

Yoga at Work

Yoga for Busy People

REDCAP

LOVE IS ALWAYS THE ANSWER

*My Survival Through the Holocaust
and Spiritual Journey with
Mrs. Irina Tweedie*

MIRIAM FREEDMAN

Lemon Soul

Published by Lemon Soul
2–10 Baron Street, London, N1 9LL
Lemon Soul is a registered imprint of 2Simple Publishing Ltd
Company number 08608270

Formerly published by Blue Dolphin Publishing
P.O. Box 8, Nevada City, CA 95959

ISBN: 978-1-57733-286-2 paperback
ISBN: 978-1-57733-460-6 e-book

Cover art: Portion of a thirty-foot mural
by Angela Sillars in Ibiza

This book is dedicated to
My beloved parents
My brother Marci
My sister Noemi
Lennie, my dear late husband
Martin and Allison, my children,
and grandchildren, Hannah and Freya,
with love

Contents

List of Illustrations

Foreword

IT IS A GREAT HONOUR and a pleasure for me to say a few
words about Miriam, who has a very special place in
my heart, and this wonderful book that documents her
spiritual journey through life.

I consider myself a very ordinary person who is
still practicing the path shown by my revered guru and
father, Mahatma Radha Mohan Lal Ji, through remem-
brance of Almighty God and service to humanity.

I can still remember the day when Mrs. Irina Tweedie came to my father from London, England, a country
with a totally different culture to ours. She not only
became one of his closest disciples, but remained with
him until he left for his heavenly abode. Mrs. Tweedie
was a staunch devotee of my father and spread his path
throughout the entire Western world.

Miriam, like Mrs. Tweedie, is also a staunch devotee
of my father's path through being one of Mrs. Tweedie's
closest associates. Miriam has devoted her life to this
path. Like Mrs. Tweedie before, Miriam came to India
to reconnect herself to the roots of my father's teaching.

I am very aware that Miriam had a challenging
childhood, and I have been humbled by how she has

been able to use this timeless spiritual teaching to overcome severe trauma.

I am confident that this book will be of great benefit to all who read it. I hope that the wisdom it contains will guide people towards their spiritual goals.

My heartiest congratulations and deepest blessings to Miriam for this good work.

Ravindra Nath
Eldest son of Mahatma Radha Mohan Laliji

Preface

THIS BOOK IS A GEM. It begins with the harrowing story of a little girl named Miriam (née Eva Mannheimer) in a small town in Slovakia during World War II. She and her family are hiding from the Nazis in a minute space behind a partition in a large apartment block. The place is crawling with Germans all trying to find the tiny remnant of Jews they knew must be somewhere in the building. A sneeze, a cough, the smallest movement of the girl could bring instant death to all concerned. Yet, they managed to survive, five adults and three children, with the help of the caretaker of the block and his family. Then the war ends. They have to hide again, this time from the Russian army which "liberated" the town, only to loot it and rape any woman that could be found.

The girl escapes death, but not tragedy. She discovers that her beloved father, a sister and brother, all have been killed, not long before the end of the war. Fortunately another sister was able to escape to Palestine before the Holocaust began. The remnants of the family are reunited. Miriam is now eleven years old and has to start the arduous journey of learning a new language and new culture. But she accomplishes the task and begins to love her adopted country with all its tensions.

She grows up and finds work as a teacher. Then she is asked by the Jewish Agency to go to Belfast as the first representative of Israel in Northern Ireland. She agrees, all the more so because she longs for space and to expand her life. There she finds love, a young actor named Lennie, and starts her own family. But being financially cramped they move to London where she discovers a new love, Yoga. It renews her wish to unfurl her limbs (still psychically constricted by the terrible time curled up behind the partition) and to breathe freely.

She soon establishes herself as an expert practitioner and teacher. Still something is missing. Then she is told about a Russian lady, Mrs. Irina Tweedie, a noted Sufi mystic, who was featured in a TV documentary on meditation and spirituality. "All I could see were Mrs. Tweedie's eyes—two blue eyes that were like an ocean of love. I might have fainted or been transported inside my mind because for a while, I didn't understand what she was saying." Later she learns that the core of Sufi teaching is the human heart. It is the centre of divine mystery and the Sufi quest which is open to seekers of all religions. Miriam is desperate to find Mrs. Tweedie, but she was not on the phone and her address was not listed anywhere. She did not realise that in the Sufi tradition it is not the student who finds the teacher, but the teacher who finds the student.

Eventually this happened and Miriam began a life-long embrace of Mrs. Tweedie and her master *Bhai Sahib*, also known as Guruji. This book is a long, loving story of their relationships, sometimes close, sometime fractious, as well as a superb exposition of their ideas. It describes how Mrs. Tweedie and Guruji came to be taken into Miriam's heart.

Towards the end of her account Miriam relates many extraordinary dreams, how she sails through time and space, to achieve the pinnacle of spiritual experiences. The book is the story of near death and redemption which, in part, is still happening.

Dr. Joseph Berke
January 2015

Acknowledgments

To Carole Brockbank, Nigel Lesmoir-Gordon and Philip Appleby for spending considerable time researching, compiling and working on the book. Without their help and encouragement the book would not have been finished. I am in deepest debt to them. I also want to thank Margaret Sampson, who was such an inspiration to me and who supported me always. Also my very dear friend Joan Margalith, who spent time working on my dreams. She helped and encouraged me throughout the whole project. Thank you, Joan. I love you. I would also like to mention the support I have had from John Clowes. My heartfelt thanks to my Paul Clemens, of Blue Dolphin Publishing for believing in my book. Thank you Sheila Griffin for always being there for me and Lily Corbett for her help and support. Ginger Gilmour, who is special to me and very dear to my heart. I must also thank Pat Brock for kindly giving me permission to use her own personal collection of Mrs. Tweedie's sayings and aphorisms. Dr. Joseph Berke and Shree Berke, who are my dear friends. My dear good friend Prof. Loknath Sriparavastu (USA), who accompanied me on my travels in India.

Guruji's son, Ravindra Nath, for telling me stories about his father and for carrying on his work in India. He, like his father, is a very special and evolved spiritual soul.

Above all I have to thank my beloved teacher Irina Tweedie. My gratitude and love will always be with her for giving me this unforgettable experience.

With many thanks to all my friends who were part of my process.

LOVE IS ALWAYS THE ANSWER

CHAPTER ONE

The Flower of Nitra

Na Nitrianska moste
fialocka rastie
nikto ju tam nezalienva
ona sama rastie

ked ja tade pojdem zalievat ju budem
a ked sa me zazelena ja ju trhavat budem

Near Nitrianska bridge
Grows a little violet.
No one there waters her,
She grows on her own.

When I walk by, I will water her.
She will grow to bloom
and I will pick her.

AUTUMN 1938

I AM MIRIAM FREEDMAN and I am Czechoslovakian. My ancestors had lived in Slovakia for hundreds of years following the Spanish Inquisition. I was born in Bratislava, the capital of Slovakia, which had previously been part of the Austro-Hungarian Empire. It was a university

Nitra Castle

city with a presidential palace, a famous theological college, wide tree-lined boulevards, department stores, smart boutiques and a thriving cultural life. The Jewish community was strong and well integrated within this lively, modern metropolis. My family was orthodox, but even so at Christmas my father would put a stocking hanging in the window full of presents. He wanted us to enjoy the day as our neighbours did.

Before war broke out, life in our comfortable apartment at 12, Suchamito, Bratislava was happy and secure. My father, Solomon Mannheimer, was one of twelve children. My mother, Olga Paskus, was one of seven children. It was a family joke that our relatives were so numerous it would be impossible for us all to be together in one house at the same time.

On Saturdays we went to Synagogue and afterwards we ate at a Jewish restaurant in the city. In the summer we often picnicked in the parks or in the surrounding hills.

My relationship with my father was special. I was the youngest in the family and he spoiled me, bringing me chocolates and bananas when he returned from his trips away. Because there were so many women in our house, I adored him and my brother—the two powerful men in my life. We often walked along the banks of the Danube. He told me wonderful stories about how our lives would be transformed when the Messiah would come to lead us to the Holy Land. I was a dreamy child and my father's stories were full of love and hope so his vision of the future sat comfortably with me and made sense. I can never forget how much he loved us. I thought I was the apple of his eye and I loved him.

Until I was about four years old our lives continued in much the same way. Father went out each day to the

Miriam and her sisters Noemi and Edith

textile factory and occasionally traveled away from home. When he returned from these trips, his private conversations with my mother increased. Although I was only a little girl and only four years old, I sensed that something was wrong. I could see how troubled he was, even though I was too young to understand what was going on.

On 29th September 1938 the British Prime Minister Neville Chamberlain met with Adolf Hitler and the leaders of France and Italy in Munich to sign an agreement, which stipulated that Czechoslovakia must cede Sudeten territory to Germany. The Czechoslovakian government was neither invited nor consulted but, under pressure from Britain and France, completely capitulated on 30th September and committed to abide by the agreement.

The French, unable to face up to Germany alone, took its lead from Chamberlain. Adolf Hitler had convinced Chamberlain that the grievances of the Sudeten Germans were justified and that Hitler had only limited intentions. On 5th October 1938 Edvard Beneš resigned as President of Czechoslovakia, eventually forming a government in exile in London. He realized that the fall of Czechoslovakia was a *fait accompli*. German occupation of the Sudetenland would be completed by 10th October.

Our life began to change as the shadow of anti-Semitism spread gradually across our country. I felt that many changes were taking place, but I was a very young child and I didn't understand what was going on. As I was the youngest, my parents didn't explain to me why we had to move or why each time we moved our new home was less comfortable than the last. With each move we became poorer and more dispossessed. It took my father a few years to fully understand what was going on. Like so many others, he didn't comprehend the enormity of what was to come.

When we moved to Judenstrasse, the Jewish district, I began to witness random acts of violence against anyone who was believed to be Jewish. Now my parents finally understood the danger we were in.

I remember walking with my father by the Danube and in the park, looking for my eldest sister Barbara (Bracha), who left Slovakia on the last ship to Palestine in 1939 via Trieste, and I hadn't understood she would not be coming back. She was the lucky one.

On another occasion I walked on my own to the Danube, hoping to spot my sister's ship. A soldier came up to me and shouted, "Jews are not allowed here." I was puzzled: How did he know I was Jewish? I thought it must be my black eyes and, even though my mother had told me how beautiful my black eyes were, I remember trying to wash them with soap to make them lighter.

In September 1941 the *Jewish Code* was passed and my father had to give up his position in the textile business. Jews were segregated in every way, excluded from

Barbara

the world of business and the professions and forced to find manual work. Jewish children were taken out of regular schools. Eventually we had to wear the yellow Star of David wherever we went. I was a rebel, and as my star was pinned on, I didn't always wear it when I went out. Of course I didn't tell anyone about this.

My parents decided to move to Nitra, a town about 40 kilometres from Bratislava in the lowlands of the Danube where my mother's family lived. We believed we would be safe there. The last home we shared as a family was in the district of Podzamska Ulica 28 in Nitra. The Jewish centre, which wasn't very far from where we lived, was called *Vatican*. Our standard of living had dropped dramatically and our accommodation was reduced to just two rooms. One of these was a kitchen where we kept our bedding. We shared a courtyard and outside toilet with several other families.

It is strange to recall now, but when the German Youth movement began arriving in our town, I stood in the street admiring all the children, who smiled, sang, and waved at us. Innocently I waved back. Everyone welcomed them and I joined in, although a part of me was trying to understand what their arrival really meant. We lived near a park where they used to exercise and I remember trying to join them to play and they asked me what my name was and when I told them, "Eva Mannheimer." They said, "You have a German name and yet you have black eyes," but still they played with me. Shortly after this our Jewish school was closed and people started to *disappear*. My own family began to disintegrate.

Our cottage had wooden shutters, which my mother kept closed in the evenings to protect us from drunken, marauding gangs throwing bricks and bottles, who regularly visited areas where they thought that Jews were living. There was a lot of fear and people continued to disappear. Were they kidnapped? The only certainty was that they were gone and they never came back. I was bewildered. I had nothing to hold onto. We lived in constant fear of our lives and there was nothing I could do. It was horrific. As a child I saw so much suffering... pregnant women beaten up, soldiers marching up and down the Jewish quarters just taking people away.

Then things became even worse. We were fearful every time we left the cottage. We started using passages and alleyways to avoid the main streets in order to move around in relative safety to buy food and visit our relatives. Despite these precautions, we were regularly attacked by hooligans. Many of the youths responsible for these attacks were barely teenagers themselves and lived in nearby streets.

My sister Noemi and my brother Marci Martin were sent to our relatives in Hungary. My parents hoped that they would be safer there. We don't know exactly what happened to Noemi but we believe that she tried to come back to us. We aren't sure. She may have died on one of the infamous death marches. Marci was safe in Hungary for a while. Boys of his young age were sent to labour camps, but our relatives saved him from this fate for a while. When the situation in Hungary deteriorated and things became bad, Marci tried to come home, but was caught at the border and sent to a concentration camp. We never saw him again.

After Marci and Noemi had left us, the open abuse of Jews intensified even more, if that can be believed! New laws were introduced, which allowed for the confiscation of money and property. My parents lost all their savings. Professional people were forced to take whatever work they could get to support their families.

After the war we heard horrific tales about atrocities that had occurred in other parts of Europe. Men, women and children had been burnt to death in a synagogue. Others had been forced to dig their own graves before they were executed. At this time we heard only rumours. These horrors had not yet reached into and been played out in Czechoslovakia. We waited and we feared the worst. We were powerless.

My sisters, Edith and Gertie, and I said our prayers and listened silently as our parents discussed in hushed voices all the possible ways to get away from the nightmare. Their opportunity for escape evaporated with their dwindling resources.

At this time reports of Jews being sent to labour camps in Poland were rumoured. The Jewish community was seized by panic and was in a state of terror. This terrible fear was also felt by many Gentiles loyal to the Jews. Many Jews worked for them and their families had grown very close.

By 1944, the unimaginable had become the reality. The authorities knew exactly where every Jewish family lived and how many people were in each household. German soldiers, accompanied by the Hlinka Guard, carried out regular house-to-house searches to capture all the men and young boys and send them to labour camps. They came to our cottage to search for my father, shouting in my face, "Where is your father?" I screamed, shook my fists at them and told them, "I don't know where he is." They didn't find him this time.

My Aunt Ela's husband, Miklos, was an accountant at a mill in the town and he had many contacts including a man named George Hoffman, who belonged to the Hlinka Guards. When the rounding up of Jews for transportation started, George warned my aunt and uncle. His fiancé was employed by my Aunt and, although he worked for the Party, he was their friend and he remained loyal to them. All our names were on the list for transportation. It was George's plan to have my sister Edith declared medically unfit to travel due to typhus. This saved our family from almost certain death in the camps. If you contracted typhus in those days, you usually died. Any contact with a sufferer had to be avoided at all costs. An epidemic could spread rapidly. George arranged for a doctor to sign a certificate for us, confirming the disease. A note was pinned to our door, notifying everyone that there was typhus in the house. People were frightened and, as hoped, they stayed away.

Then a further order came from the town hall, decreeing that all Jews had to assemble in *Vatican*, near the train station, to be transported to the camps. The Hlinka Guard and George accompanied us. When we reached the train station, he informed the officer in charge that there was typhus in our family and presented the doctor's certificate. We were refused permission to travel and told to return to our home—it was a miracle! Our family was saved once more and I am able to tell my story because of the intervention of a Nazi party organizer. He was a moral man. His action went some way to later restoring my faith in human nature.

After the trains left we had to continue with the pretence of my sister's illness for several weeks, as she couldn't be seen to recover too quickly. Slowly a fragile kind of "normality" began to return to the town—before the next wave of transportations. We heard later that when the transportation of Jews to the camps started, the Kings of Bulgaria and Denmark protested, as did the citizens of Holland, Italy and Greece, but sadly the Slovakian authorities were complicit with the Nazis and willingly agreed to give up their Jewish citizens. Eventually a decree was issued, which ordered the removal of every Jew from Nitra. It was all so final and so terrible. Overnight chaos and fear engulfed the town. Everyone adopted "fancy dress." Some people dressed like Germans, some like peasants, others like Christian clergy—anything to disguise themselves and save their lives. Anyone who could get hold of a horse and cart bundled their few possessions and children onto it and fled.

Nobody knew how long this madness and danger would last. Everything was kept secret by the town officials and the Hlinka Guards and it wasn't until the decrees were issued that anyone knew anything.

Outside Slovakia nobody knew or understood what was going on. All travel had long since been prohibited to Jews. The only certain thing was that people who disappeared were *never* seen again.

On the day of the final decree—the day that Jews were told they could no longer remain in their homes— my father left early in the morning as usual to work in the brick factory on the other side of town across the river Nitra. When the siren sounded, calling all Jews to assemble at the railway tracks for the final transportation, my poor mother didn't know what to do. She started running hysterically up and down, clasping

Gerti and me by the hand. Edith went to some friends to find out what was going on and we never saw her again until the end of the war. We wanted to cross the river to find my father but a guard had told my mother that if she crossed the river there was no guarantee that we could come back, so we did not go. My mother then searched for her sister Ela, who she thought may be in a block of flats belonging to the Mill where uncle Miklos worked. We walked up and down outside the building, my mother constantly calling out "Ela, Ela." Suddenly we heard Ela calling "Olga! Olga!" My mother stopped running and we went into a ground floor flat where she, my aunts Lily, Seren and Ela's husband, Miklos, and my cousin Robi were hiding. They opened the door for us and we stumbled inside. And so began our life in hiding.

The arrow on the right indicates the window of the flat where the family hid

We stayed out of sight in the flat for several days while the German soldiers and the Hlinka Guard continued to search for Jews. We didn't know what to do or what was going to happen to us.

We didn't get colds or temperatures, but I do remember breaking out in boils all over my body. The puss had to be squeezed out. I think this must have been caused by the relentless stress of our ceaseless state of fear and lack of food. We couldn't call a doctor. It was too great a risk. I recovered slowly without any medication.

A few days later, we saw our father standing alone on the other side of the street, unshaven, without a hat and dressed in his working clothes. He was looking for us. My mother started to put on her shoes to go into the street to save him. My uncle forbade it. He told her that if she went out she couldn't come back in. If she did, she might be seen and then they'd all be discovered. It wasn't safe. My mother had to decide to make contact and risk everything or not. She decided not to. She put down her shoes and moved away from the window.

I'll never know exactly why she did this, why my father didn't cross the road and enter the flat, or why he wasn't let in. We were eight people—five adults and three children—surely there would have been room for one more. I don't think anybody would have recognized him. I never saw my father again.

Our hiding place in the flat was perilous. Days and nights were punctuated by the continuous sound of blaring loudspeakers, booming out the message that anyone who hid a Jew placed his life in jeopardy. For every Jew handed over to the authorities a substantial reward would be paid.

Unknown to us, Uncle Miklos and Aunt Ela Fisher had already made a plan. In the event of the unimaginable catastrophe of the total expulsion of all Jews from Nitra, they were going to hide in the flats which the mill owned for their employees, until they could escape.

Our protector William Gavalovich, who worked at the mill with my uncle Miklos, had already taken at least four good people into his confidence before the fateful day dawned: his fiancée Helena Gavalova, Witek Perni, the caretaker and Maria his wife who was just twenty-five and the mill director. When they hid us, they put themselves in terrible danger. I can never fully express my gratitude and admiration for these people. They were brave heroes.

William decided it would be safer for us all to move to the second floor of the mill apartments in one of the vacant bachelor flats. There were about thirty flats in total, a mixture of single and family accommodation. We made our way up there in the dead of night.

We remained in hiding there until the war ended. We had only the clothes on our backs—nothing else— no books, no toys. Our new hiding place in the tiny flat consisted of one room, a small entrance hall and a bathroom with a toilet. We sat in utter silence in this tiny room—in *utter* silence. We children were not allowed to open our mouths—ever! In fact no one spoke. We were all too frightened. I don't remember saying anything or having a proper conversation during the entire time we were incarcerated. We couldn't even sneeze or clear our throats. We all lost our voices. Eventually we couldn't walk properly either. Our circulation had been affected by the lack of mobility. Along with my sister and cousin we may have been seen as a burden.

Ela and Miklos Fisher

*William Gavalovic, Helena Gallova, the Mill Director and
Miklos Fisher*

From time to time we had to stand up to stretch our legs and walk, but as the building was not solidly constructed and our footsteps might be heard, we had to wait for our friend, Witek Perni, to signal to us when the people above and below had left for work and it was safe to move around. We tried to exercise. It was very difficult. I used to peep at the children laughing and playing in the street outside and I yearned to be one of them. They were living in another world—in a parallel universe.

Christmas was coming and Witek told his little daughter Alzebeta about us. We all knew her as Duly. She was the same age as me. It was a most dangerous thing to do, but she had to know, as she'd started asking questions such as why there was so much cooking and laundry being done in the house. She must have been tempted many times in school to tell her friends that she knew a secret nobody else did. But her father trusted her and, as it turned out, justifiably took her into his confidence. My Christmas present that year was that we were allowed to play together for a short time. Duly brought me some toys and a book and I was so very excited to be with someone my own age again. As we started playing, she asked me what I would like to do. My one and only dream was to run in a field. I had not been able to walk outside for many months. So I replied, "I would like to run. When the war is over I will race you and I will run so fast that you will never catch me!"

The reality was very different. After the war my legs were so swollen from sitting still I could hardly stand up. I made up for this later in my life by becoming very active in sports, especially running.

We began to sense that there might be an informer living in the apartments. Our main worry was that the people who lived above us and below us were becoming suspicious. William and Perni decided to confide in the family who lived next door to us. The husband didn't want to tell his wife or children about us for fear of placing them in danger, so he sent them away to the country to stay with relatives. There were rumours that other Jews might be hiding in the building and the Germans started to conduct routine searches.

Beneath our apartment block there was a basement area divided into sections where coal was stored for central heating and where the residents could do their laundry in the washing machines provided. Each section had a lock and every resident had their own space in the basement where they could store their suitcases, old furniture and barrels of preserves. Some people went to the basement to do carpentry and other repairs.

The Germans intensified their house to house searches and Perni decided to create a second hiding place for us in the basement—a hiding place of last resort.

He cut a hole in one of the section walls like a fireplace. It was about two metres by two metres and a metre or so high. He disguised it well by stacking jars of pickles and jams in front of it. Air could circulate between the jars.

Whenever there was an emergency and another search was imminent, Perni and Gavalovich would each seize one of my aunts and my mother, then stagger, apparently drunk, down the back stairs with them to the safety of our hiding place. Sometimes, they pretended to be lovers, frivolous and light-hearted. My sister Gerti and cousin Robi were bundled up inside sheets or rolled-up carpets and carried down. As I was so small, I was carried in a laundry basket.

We lay crouched together on the floor of the fireplace, all eight of us like sardines, covering ourselves with old eiderdowns and sacking, and lying completely still until the danger passed. When we left the upstairs flat for the basement, all the furniture in the flat would be removed. Dirt and excrement would be smeared across the floors and walls to convince the Germans that nobody could possibly live there.

Life in the basement was absolutely terrible. There were eight of us—five adults and three children—jammed together in a tiny hole with barely enough air to breathe. I remember them saying "Move, move," so I was squashed up against a pipe. It made me want to

The entrance to the basement hiding place is marked with an arrow

Inside the hiding place, which was just 6 feet x 8 feet

cry but I was not allowed to cry. We had a bucket in case we needed to go to the toilet urgently. I can't remember *ever* going to the toilet when we were hidden in that basement. The fact is that when you don't eat proper meals for a long time, you don't need to go to the toilet so often.

Next door was a large washroom with a manhole, which was sometimes used as a toilet instead of the bucket when we were sure no one was around. We washed our faces and hands with a few drops of water from the stand pipe. Next to our hiding place was a room which had previously been used for heavy storage and was also commandeered by the Germans to use as a gym. Soldiers arrived at any time during the day to exercise. Sometimes up to twenty soldiers at a time would exercise, and for several hours we lay huddled in total silence nearby, listening to them shouting and talking. We even controlled the sound of our breathing by covering our mouths with our eiderdowns. We were only the width of a brick away from discovery! These were the most terrifying hours I can remember.

Then something happened that changed our routine and our suspicions about informers in the building grew stronger. Witek changed the lock on the flat to make it more secure and in case the owner came back. We knew we could rely utterly on Witek. He put his own life in danger helping us. In truth he took as many risks as we did—many more in fact than we were aware of at the time.

One day shortly after this Witek rushed upstairs to warn us we were in grave danger. A drunken German officer had walked into the building, shouting that he knew Jews were hiding here and that no matter how long it took, he would find them. Witek told us that he didn't think he could do anything more for us, as the stairway route to the basement was blocked by soldiers. We would all be seen if we left the flat. He suggested we commit suicide by turning on the gas ring. With hindsight, even if we had done this, it would have taken several hours for the gas to take effect, and before that our neighbours would most certainly have been alerted by the smell. He said that he would burn our bodies in the basement incinerator. He said goodbye to us and told us we should pray.

Uncle Miklos pointed out that since there were about thirty flats in the block it would take some time for the soldiers to reach us.

I knew that I didn't want to die. I told everyone that if Uncle Miklos turned on the gas ring, I would jump out of the window, giving away the hiding place. The adults realized that I meant it and abandoned the plan. Someone suggested hiding behind the wardrobe, but the smell of our bodies in the room would have given us away. So in the end we just sat there, huddled together, holding hands and praying, waiting to be taken. We surrendered to the idea of being caught. We accepted it. We had been in hiding for ten months at this point and the prospect of freedom through death seemed almost sweet and acceptable. We spent many hours sitting there, crying and desperately fearful. Eventually we heard the scraping of German boots as the soldiers approached the door to our apartment.

But what we hadn't bargained for was the resourcefulness of Witek's wife Maria. She and her mother had plied the German officer with schnapps and we only heard the sound of laughter and joking as the officer came closer. We were very puzzled.

Witek slowly inserted the old key into the lock. We listened to it rattling as he manoeuvred it from side to side, struggling to open the door. To our amazement, we heard Witek say, "I think you must have made a mistake. We have just left this apartment. Why do you want to go back again?" Somehow Witek convinced the officer that he had made an error and the drunken man accepted this. He walked away. This was a most powerful and almost unbelievable incident. The officer entered every apartment except for ours. When Witek returned, he told us that the officer was satisfied there weren't any Jews in the flats. We had survived again. It was truly a miracle. After the war we discovered there were in fact several other Jews hiding in the building—just like us.

CHAPTER TWO

The Liberation

SPRING 1945

IN THE SPRING OF 1945 we were still incarcerated in the flat. Witek brought us news of the Russian advance into Slovakia and we again retreated to the basement. Other residents from the flats started to use the basement to hide from the bombing, so it was filling up with people. It was harder for Witek to bring us food. He used to sneak down at night and leave us what he could. Our money had run out a long time ago, but my uncle had given a promise to pay back everything that was owed for food and other things after the war and he kept his promise.

The Germans were starting to retreat, but a lot of Slovaks continued to cooperate with them. It was still very dangerous. Eventually the Russian forces crossed the River Nitra and prepared to enter the town. Our building was close to the river and it was one of the first that the Russian officers entered.

Most people assumed that, when the liberation came, it would be a good thing, although initially things were still very difficult. A Russian officer discovered us huddled in our hiding place in the basement. Witek told us not to speak German. We tried to tell the officer in Slovakian about what had been happening and the terrible peril we had been in. But the officer knew absolutely nothing about the fate of the Jews and couldn't understand the situation. These soldiers were in the Russian regular army and they knew nothing about Hitler and the "Final Solution." The officer patted me on the head and gave me a sweet just like my father. Then he and Witek spoke together in Russian as we discovered Witek was a Communist supporter. The officer explained that the Russian occupying force hadn't seen a woman for a long time. He told us to stay in hiding until the troops had left, and that my aunts should disguise themselves as old women if they had to leave the building, as he couldn't guarantee their safety. In the months after the liberation, most of the women in the town were either pregnant or had been raped. Even women of seventy and eighty were raped by the Russian troops. Now we had to hide from our "liberators," and our difficult life in the basement continued for a while. Though the Germans had been defeated, killed, or had run away, we were still very fearful. The Russian soldiers now occupied the building and our town instead of the Germans.

The bombing and the shooting continued constantly day and night for a while. I was very frightened by the sound of Russian planes attacking the town. The River Nitra was just twenty yards wide, but many of the advancing troops were very primitive and were completely ignorant of where they were. They thought that they had just crossed the River Volga and so believed that they were still on Russian soil!

When it was safe, we left the basement. We had been in hiding for such a long time so we knew very little about what had happened in the rest of the country and in the world. Our cottage had been bombed and looted. Our Slovak neighbours had been concerned that we might return and hadn't taken everything, so our furniture was still there. It was a truly extraordinary experience to walk outside again after such a long time in hiding. We repressed all our emotions, feelings, and thoughts to start with. After a while I was able to begin to understand what had happened, and then I started school again.

The United Nations Refugee Organisation (UNRO) opened an office in the town. We found out through UNRO that my father and brother Marci had both died in the camps and that my sister, Noemi, had possibly perished on one of the infamous Death Marches. There was no news of Edith. We were not sure what had happened to her. Gradually we found out that only about 80 Jews had survived in the *entire* city of Nitra plus the eight of us.

Initially we stayed with Aunt Boszi and Uncle Hugo in their big house in Nitra. After some time we moved what remained of our furniture into an empty apartment on the old street in Podzamska where we used to live.

We were told by a neighbor that the day after my poor father stood in the street calling for my mother he went away and hid in the fields. He had no money and didn't know what to do. At night he came back to the cottage to sleep, waiting and hoping for help that never came. Somebody informed on him and the Hlinka

Guard came for him. They dragged him out of the cottage and sent him to Ebensee, which was an Austro-Hungarian concentration camp.

We were told two conflicting stories concerning what happened to Marci.

The first of these was that he had been caught near the border with Hungary, trying to re-enter Slovakia on his own and rejoin the family. He was by then a strong eighteen year old and valuable as a labourer. We were informed that it was very likely that he managed to get himself into

Gerty, my mother Olga, Edith and Miriam after the war

the Russian sector of the Ebonsee concentration camp, which was considered safer with less harsh conditions. Some Jews did this, believing that, when the allies advanced, there would be negotiations between the Russians and the Nazis, resulting in their exchange release. Marci was old enough to understand all of this. It influenced his decision to contrive his imprisonment with the Russians. In this version of events, Marci was seen alive a few days before the liberation. The Germans in their defeat simply didn't know what to do with the prisoners. When the officer in charge of the camp learned that the Russian troops were advancing, he ordered all the inmates to be shot, and this was how my brother died.

The other version of events concerning Marci was that he died in the same camp as our father, which was Mauthausen concentration camp. In this version,

Marci was transported to Ebensee where he met our father and gave him some bread through the barbed wire fence. From there, both were transported probably at different times to Mauthausen, which was one of the worst camps, and where they both perished three months before the end of the war.

CHAPTER THREE

To Palestine and Security

MY ELDEST SISTER BARBARA (Bracha) had moved to Palestine in 1939, and after the war she sent us an affidavit to join her in Palestine. My mother had discovered through UNRO that my father, my sister, and brother had died. So there was no reason for us to remain in Slovakia any longer. We were desperate to get away from Nitra and reach Palestine so we travelled by train to Paris, passing through Bratislava. Before the war my mother had always wanted to see Paris, but she could not have known it would be under such circumstances. Nevertheless we walked our feet off and saw as much of the city as we could. I don't remember much of this time. The important thing is that we were together. In Paris and Marseilles we were given a great welcome and were treated like heroes by the local people. It was an exhausting and intense journey.

In Marseilles we boarded a ship called the Annapolis sailing to Palestine. It was a Greek vessel and it was very basic. The Captain was fully aware of what was going on. We were travelling legally but not all the passengers had permits like us. Most of the passengers were soldiers of the Czechoslovakia Brigade, who were going to Palestine at that time to help fight for the Jewish cause. At this time Palestine was under British mandate. The settlement process was complicated and there were many political problems between the British and the Jewish settlers and the resistance groups.

When we docked in Palestine, it was very exciting and a little frightening. A curfew had been imposed and a siren was blaring through the port, which awoke terrifying memories in me. The British were looking for rebel organisations opposed to the regime. As we stepped onto land, I kissed the ground. It was holy ground to me. My father used to say to me, "If you go to Palestine the Messiah will arrive." It was a special and highly significant moment in my life and I remembered his words. I was struck immediately by the heat and the overwhelming blueness of the cloudless sky.

We moved into my sister's flat in Jerusalem which was very small, a bedsit in fact. My mother could not afford to keep us, so the Jewish Agency helped to find me a family to live with in a village called Kafar Haroi. This family did not understand my needs. They did not appreciate that I was very young, that I was damaged, and that I needed nurturing love. Sadly it was not forthcoming. I had to help around the house after school. I spoke no Hebrew and I was very lonely. My mother saw how unhappy I was when she came to visit me and it upset her. She arranged for me to go to a boarding school near Haifa called Kfar Hanoar Hadati.

I was now eleven years old and travelled to Kfar Hasidim alone by bus and then walked to the school at Kfar Hanoar Hadati carrying my few possessions. Looking back I can see that I was very brave to face up to all these things alone—absolutely all alone. Many children arrived there at the same time. I found the office, announced my name and a "carer" came and showed me around the school and my dormitory to share with three other girls.

My mother was in Jerusalem and I didn't go home for a very long time. The war was on in Palestine. There was no telephone, no vacation and very little contact with my mother. I missed home. The British withdrew and the war started between the Arabs and the Israelis. I feared that my mother and sisters might be killed. My mother contacted me after I had been at the school for some time. I was very happy to hear from her; it was a great relief. She told me she would see me soon. I

Miriam with friends at boarding school

*Miriam with her
closest friend Ajala*

did not tell her I had been unhappy.

At the school, although I was a lonely and insecure child, I managed to make some friends (who remain my dear friends to this day). I used to wander alone through the mountains. I asked God, "Why am I here? Why did my saintly father, my brother, my sister and all those wonderful people have to die? What is the purpose of my life?" The answer came back to me somehow, "To do some work." But what that work was I had no idea.

My sister Barbara was living in Tiberius with her doctor husband. My other sister, Edith, was living on a kibbutz called Nir-David where she lived for years and eventually met her husband, Israel Glazer, whom I respected and to some extent he replaced my father and my brother. He bought me my first recorder and I still have it and treasure it. When they came to visit me at the school, it was such a treat to be with my family. It was a religious school and very regimented. It had a very impressive reputation and was considered to be a good mixed school with many teachers from European backgrounds. I observed all the rituals of our faith. We were looked after by a matron and she was very strict. She seemed to have no understanding of our needs and we were never given any love, so we did our best to comfort each other. We all had crushes on our teachers. It was a kind of compensation and a form of transference. I was particularly taken by my gym teacher and consequently became a good sportswoman. I was also keen on my young physics teacher who was very good looking.

Of course, being far too shy, I had no boyfriends though some of the other girls had boyfriends. My father and my brother were my idols and none of the boys at the school measured up to my expectations of what a man should be. Friendships were hard for me to forge.

The society we lived in was in fact greatly influenced by socialism and socialist ideals. The first Jewish settlers in Palestine were pioneers who came from Russia and other Eastern European countries. As it happened, my school was also open to socialist ideas and many of us thought that our new country would be a socialist state.

Miriam with friends at boarding school

This changed as soon as Israel was declared a state by the United Nations.

My school had a good library with a wide range of books, which included a lot of Russian literature. Books were my best friends and I read many Russian classics: Tolstoy, Gogol and Dostoyevsky, and many others at the age of just fifteen. I read all the time to fill the emptiness and to dull the pain of my loneliness.

After a year I started to have a more interesting time at school. I had a garden plot in my name and I enjoyed being with animals. I was good at sports and was asked to join the handball and running teams.

The war of independence was underway and we children did our best to help in the effort by running messages and working on the land. I stayed at the boarding school until I was seventeen. I had learned to speak Hebrew fairly fluently. It had taken me a year to master it. We all had to learn the language as we had come from a variety of different European countries—Czechoslovakia, Romania, Germany, Poland, Belgium, France, Italy, and other countries. At that time many people believed that the country would be influenced by communism. When the United Nations assembly voted to accept Israel's independence state in 1947, the first country to recognise it was the Soviet Union, the second country the United States.

Although I was a difficult and rebellious teenager, I did manage to win a scholarship to study in Jerusalem at Efrata College where I spent three years and trained to be a junior teacher. I lived with my mother and one sister in a bedsit in Jerusalem. It was truly wonderful to be reunited with them although it was a difficult time for all of us. My mother found it difficult to pick up a new language and she had very little money. She worked as a cook for a member of Parliament and was an excellent cook even though she hadn't trained professionally. She insisted that we all learn a profession. My eldest sister worked as a physiotherapist and later in a bank and obtained an MA degree in German literature. My second sister was a librarian and my third sister, who was very good with her hands, became an artist and worked in a craft centre.

We had a limited variety to eat in those days. Food was rationed, but my mother managed to cook superb meals with very little. She made the most wonderful pancakes from dried eggs, and vegetable pies and risotto from the most basic ingredients. Her cooking was so good that all my friends loved her and visited her often to taste her food. She was very strict with us, but nonetheless I did have a few boyfriends when I was in college. She always worried about me and didn't approve!

At age twenty I passed my exams and was qualified to teach. Then I was called up for army service. Being religious, I was presented with the choice of going into the regular army for two years or working in a new border settlement. I chose the latter.

It was thrilling to serve my country. I worked with young immigrant children from Morocco, Iraq and Kurdistan in Parvanot near Emek Beit Shan and I lived in a kibbutz named Shluchot.

I had to cycle several miles to work every day through a very rugged area, which I would never dare to do today. Looking back it could have been very dangerous, but I was young and fearless and thought

*Miriam before she
joined the army*

With friends in Israel

nothing of it at the time. I didn't have much choice. I had to walk or cycle.

A year later I was based in a very beautiful mountainous region in the village of Elkosh, working with more immigrant children who were finding it difficult to learn the language and integrate into the Israeli culture. I loved those children just as I loved our young country with a fierce loyalty. Israel had become a reality, and the promise to make the desert bloom was being fulfilled. I related to those children because, like them, I did not have a straightforward education.

I had lost my early years of schooling to the Nazi occupation so had to work particularly hard when I was at the boarding school in order to catch up, learning a new language and a new way of life as these children were.

On finishing my military service I found a job teaching immigrant children again in a town called Naharia near Haifa; my mother lived nearby in a village called Kiryat Samuel. By this time she had a proper apartment of her own near the sea. I managed to help my mother financially and could also afford to join folk and ballroom dancing groups. I love dancing.

I travelled by bus to work every day and sometimes I hitchhiked and would get lifts from prominent people such as Moshe Dayan and Moshe Sharet before he became Prime Minister. They didn't need security in those days. Life was very different then. It was safe for them to travel alone and to pick up hitchhikers like me. I met all kinds of people in that way and worked in Naharia for two years.

On one occasion I visited Jerusalem to meet an old friend from Dublin called Sara, whom I had met at teacher training college. I went to visit her at her home one day and she introduced me to a representative of the Jewish Agency. He told us that he was looking for someone to go to Northern Ireland to work on organizing the education of Jewish children and adults there and to promote tourism to Israel. He asked Sara if she would take the job as she came from Ireland. Sara told him that she didn't want to go and suggested to him that he send me. He interviewed me a few times and decided I was suitable for the work. I was just twenty-three and wanted to see the world so I jumped at the opportunity. Looking back, it was very bold and brave of me to take on the task but the adventure really appealed to me. I had heard of England but knew nothing of Ireland.

CHAPTER FOUR

Belfast and Lennie

WHEN THE TIME CAME FOR ME TO LEAVE ISRAEL, I said good-bye to my mother and family with great sadness. I was about to enter a new world and knew I would not see my family for some time. My mother was very concerned for me, but I wanted to travel. It was the opportunity of a lifetime.

The Jewish Agency gave me some French and English currency for the journey and informed me that I would travel alone to London from Marseilles on a ship called "The Theodor Herzl." I was to be met in Marseilles and London by representatives of the Jewish Agency.

We set sail in December 1958. On board the ship I noticed a very beautiful woman who was attracting a lot of attention. I was mesmerized by her beauty. It turned out that she had nearly become Miss Israel, coming second in the competition. Eventually I got into conversation with her and her husband Sam. She told me they were newly married, having met just three weeks ago. She asked me if I was travelling alone and I said that I was. She was surprised that such a young and pretty girl would be travelling alone and we became friendly and talked about our lives now. Among other things, I told her that when I was in the army I had met a South African man called Danny and we had fallen deeply in love. The romance was sadly very short-lived because he had to return to South Africa to finish his studies. She asked if I had any photographs of him. I had just a few shots of us taken together and I showed them to her. She was amazed and told me that she knew this man and said that he had left her to be with me. What an unbelievable coincidence! When we docked in Marseilles, although my new friends had first class train tickets, they decided to travel second class with me. It was kind of them to stay with me. We had to go via Paris and the journey to London took a long time. When we finally arrived, Sam asked me if I would like to join them at the Cumberland Hotel. It was an expensive hotel and it still is. Amazingly, I completely ignored the fact that I was supposed to be meeting the Jewish Agency representative. Somehow I put it right out of my mind. It was December and this lovely couple offered to take me to Selfridges to buy me a gift of a winter coat as it was very cold. I had a wonderful time with them sight-seeing in London and I continued to ignore the fact that I was supposed to have met the representative.

Looking back now I can hardly believe I did this. They thought I might have been kidnapped. The police and Interpol were alerted and they started to search for me. Eventually they tracked me down and the representative was furious. I was embarrassed and humiliated. I said goodbye to my friends, who were returning to their home in Florida, and I meekly went on to Belfast alone. The Agency had set up some temporary accom-

In Belfast

modation for me with a Jewish family. I stayed there for a short time then went to live in a boarding house when I started work.

I wasn't frightened; in fact I was very happy to teach and meet new people. Soon after my arrival I started the first kindergarten and organised Hebrew classes and tourism, making many friends because I was something of a celebrity being the first representative of Israel in Northern Ireland. I was interviewed by the press. It was a new and strange experience for me.

Eventually I was contacted by two Israeli representatives in the Republic of Ireland. They visited me and we became great friends. It was good for me because they were able to help me with my work as they were doing similar work in Dublin. I stayed with this couple a few times. We went on holiday together occasionally and planned programmes.

I was invited to a ball in Dublin with a friend. It was one of those dances where the women huddled in one group and the men in another. During the evening I needed to go to the toilet, but the ladies' room was upstairs and there was a group of drunken men on the stairs, who wouldn't let me through. One of them said as a joke that, if I dated him, he would let me pass. He told me he was an actor and that his name was Lennie Freedman. Although he was very good looking and charming, I didn't take to him immediately. We said goodbye and a few weeks later he told the Dublin representatives that he would like to meet me again, so they invited us both for dinner. Lennie told me he liked horse riding and asked me if I would like to go with him one day. I agreed and he taught me how to ride. We had a good time and he started to fall for me. I wasn't very interested yet, but he was persistent. He called me by phone on several occasions and eventually came to Belfast to take me out. He was clearly very interested in me, so much so, that after a very short courtship he asked if I would like to meet his parents. I was very surprised indeed by this suggestion as we had known each other for such a short time. Traditionally of course a meeting with parents indicated great interest. He was taking our relationship very seriously. He invited me to stay with his parents for a weekend. They had a nice home and Lennie's father took to me because he seldom brought female friends home. He worked in his father's business and also acted in the famous Abbey Theatre. Lennie and I shared a love of the arts and Israel.

His family was very happy that he had found a Jewish girl and so he pursued his courtship. He made me feel special and we became good friends, which developed into a deeper friendship and then he proposed. I went to visit my cousins in Switzerland en route to Israel. Lennie regularly sent me flowers and telegrams. My heart was in Israel and I wasn't sure that he was the right person for me because of our backgrounds. I was a dedicated Zionist and I loved everything about Israel, even the terrible heat. When I found out how much Lennie also loved Israel, I felt closer to him. He had lived there for a while and knew the country reasonably well, but he had difficulties with the language. He spoke only broken Hebrew.

Eventually I fell in love with him, so when he proposed to me again, my only condition was that we live in Israel for the rest of our lives. It was my real home. Lennie agreed to this condition. He was training to be a podiatrist as well as being an actor, and we thought he would easily find a job in Israel. At the end of my contract in Belfast I went back via Europe to Israel and he followed me there.

We were married in Haifa. Lennie and I loved beautiful things and we also had a shared interest in nature and wildlife.

At first Lennie was willing to do any kind of work. I still had my teaching job waiting for me. We found a beautiful fl at on Mount Carmel and Lennie auditioned to be in an Otto Preminger film called *Exodus*. Lennie was accepted because of his captivating voice and his training with the Abbey Theatre, and was offered the part of the doctor on the ship. Because we were newly

Our wedding day

married and would have to be apart for many months while he would be filming in Cyprus, I didn't want him to go, not realising what a great opportunity he would miss. I regret to this day that I did not encourage him to take this job when it was offered to him.

Lennie didn't have a steady job, and I was pregnant. Things were difficult for us; we knew I would not be able to work for much longer. We knew he could find work in London and I reluctantly agreed to return to England.

CHAPTER FIVE

Living in London

OUR FIRST CHILD WAS BORN IN DUBLIN. We stayed with Lennie's family and after six months we moved to London and found a small flat in Golders Green. Lennie was trying to establish himself and we struggled financially. He didn't make much money. Like me he was a dreamer, but he finished his training to be a podiatrist. He wanted to act and deep down he would like to have lived the life of a Bohemian artist, but that didn't work out for him. He didn't care about material things and that caused some conflict between us because we had a family to support and I had to work too. I worked as a teacher and became a head teacher. We really struggled but we were independent. Eventually I received a little compensation from the German government. It was enough for us to put down a deposit on our first house. We had saved a little money and were able to have it done up.

Martin was born a year after our marriage and we employed an *au pair* to look after him so that we could both go out to work. We had a very small mortgage and Lennie was given a pay rise. Our families were very supportive, which helped a lot. Our friends were moving on and buying bigger houses and we could see the sense in this kind of investment. We worked hard to improve our home. After about twelve years we moved to a bigger house. We didn't want to stay in the same road with our neighbourhood friends moving away.

Five years later our daughter Allison Noemi was born. I developed a very bad back pain, which I have continued to suffer from now and again to this very day. One day when I was collecting Martin from school I fell into conversation with a very lovely woman. She was always smiling and I called her "Sunshine" to myself. Her name was actually Gill Goldman. She told me that she was from Suffolk and that she was married to a South African called Maurice. He was a chemist and also a very good writer. He held free Yoga classes in the evening after he finished work. Even though I knew nothing about Yoga, I asked if I could come to one of his classes and she told me that I would be most welcome. Gill told me that Yoga would help me with my back problem so it was of great interest to me. It was all very new to me.

They lived not far from us and I went to a class with a friend of mine. They had no car or telephone and they lived in a shed at the bottom of their garden as they had turned their house into a Yoga studio. It was unbelievable. They had four children who slept there. I felt very drawn to this couple. I had never met anyone like them before and they made a deep impression on me. Every time I visited them, there was always a vegetarian meal on the table. They were a lovely family and whenever I went there for classes, I was always made very welcome. I studied hard with them and I was a

*Gill and Maurice Goldman,
my first yoga teachers*

good student. We got on well and we became friends. I adored them and wanted to be like them.

Shortly after the Six Day War in Israel, Maurice and Gill decided to move to Israel. I felt I was losing my special bond with them and I was shocked when they asked me to take over the Yoga classes. They insisted that I could handle it. I was good at Yoga but didn't feel up to this huge challenge and responsibility and didn't consider myself knowledgeable or experienced enough for the task. I knew I definitely didn't have sufficient understanding of the philosophy that lay behind the yogic practice. I had only read Swami Vishnudevananda Saraswati's book on Yoga and knew next to nothing of the philosophy behind Hatha Yoga, so I took a course at the Shivananda Centre and began to understand more deeply the true meaning of Yoga. True Yoga means the union of the lower with the higher self. I met with Swami Vishnudevananda a few times and he initiated me into Yoga. I read more on the subject and my knowledge started to build and helped me gain a firmer footing. When my friends moved to Israel, they went to live in a mountainous region in a most beautiful vegan village called Moshav Amirim, upper Gallilee. I visited there many times. It was a truly wonderful place.

I began to teach Yoga in my home in London. Before long I had to deal with more practical matters due to the trust placed in me by my friends. Swami Vishnudevananda, who lived in the USA, told his students when they visited London to come to my Yoga class.

One day I opened my door to some visitors and, when I said I was Miriam, one of my callers said she believed I was carrying the teaching of Swami Sivananda and they all bowed down on the floor in front of me, insisting I was somebody special. I was absolutely shocked by this and I told them they had got it all wrong and that like them I was just a student of Yoga. They became my students and I invited them to stay with us for a weekend which surprised them, but I wanted to show them Yoga hospitality. This encouraged me to study more myself and I went to many seminars and workshops.

CHAPTER SIX

The Unfolding

I REALIZED THAT I HAD TO ACQUIRE a much deeper knowledge of the practices and philosophy of Hatha Yoga. I started to fully appreciate that my involvement in Yoga was helping me to realize that life was truly worth living.

Over the next ten years I trained hard at Yoga and in a range of alternative and complementary therapies as well as counseling. I studied the Iyengar and Patanjali methods of Yoga.

I was initiated by Swami Vishnudevananda at five o'clock in the morning at a wonderful ceremony in Regent's Park.

I then decided to take a teacher training course in Hatha Yoga and I joined the British Wheel of Yoga where I studied for several years and I became a qualified Yoga teacher. Things were really starting to come together for me—getting better and better.

Lennie took great pride in the fact that, although I was a foreigner in a foreign country, I was making an impact in the world of yoga. I took on a large number of students and my classes were attended by forty people or more. It was impressive and I did well as a teacher owing to my earlier training.

Due to this work I really thought for a while that I had come to terms with those terrible things I had experienced as a child. Following a depression, and after I started to see a psychotherapist, I realized I had been using denial as a way of shielding myself from my past. I had not been able to look back at my childhood.

One day there was a radio programme where I heard that the BBC wanted to interview survivors of the Holocaust. I phoned in and spoke to an American journalist and she arranged to visit me for an interview. She came to my house soon after.

As I talked to her, I realized that this was the first time I had spoken to a complete stranger about my childhood. I found I was able to talk to her, and the floodgates opened and I told her of my great losses.

Unbeknownst to me she passed on my contact number to BBC2 television. A new phase of my life had begun. I had never spoken to my children about the Holocaust. I tried to protect them from the truth of this tragedy.

Time passed. On the 1st April 1995 I received a call from a man who said he was a researcher for BBC2. He asked me to participate in a VE Day documentary film. I put the phone down thinking it was an April Fool's day joke. The phone rang again, he assured me it was no joke and we had a good laugh about it. They had decided that they wanted me to be a part of their documentary to commemorate VE Day. I accepted as I knew that it was very important for me to do this.

Things escalated from there and I was contacted by the Shoah Foundation. They asked me to record a series of video interviews for the Steven Spielberg Project. The Shoah Foundation conducted 50,000 interviews in 56 countries and in 32 languages for posterity, and I wanted to record my life as part of this project.

The recordings are preserved. The interviewees included Jewish survivors, Jehovah's Witness survivors, homosexual survivors, liberators and liberation witnesses, political prisoners, rescuers, aid providers, and war crimes trials participants.

Shortly after this I was approached by the American journalist again, who told me that she wanted to take me to Slovakia to make a film about my life. In the end she did not raise the necessary funding and the project fell through. This was a big disappointment for me because many of the people who had helped me to survive were still alive. It would have been a wonderful thing to have done.

Following hard on the heels of the BBC2 interview I found these things easier to do. I shared these video interviews with my family as an education project. Several years later when the children were older, we were invited to Slovakia for me to take part in a ceremony organised by the Slovakian government and Yad Vashem of Jerusalem to honour the memory of those citizens, who had helped Jewish people during World War II. I was asked by Yad Vashem and the Israeli Ambassador to Austria, Mr. Sher, to speak before the Slovakian government in the presence of President Kovatz in the Presidential palace. It was a very great honour for me to do this. This is the speech I gave on that day:

It is a great privilege and honour for my family and myself to participate on this occasion in the presence of the Slovakian President, Michael Kovec, the Israeli Ambassador to Austria, Yoel Sher and the curator of Yad Vashem in Jerusalem, to

BOTSCHAFTER DES STAATES ISRAEL
WIEN

שגריר ישראל
וינה

Vienna, 11 August 1997

Dear Mrs. Freedman,

On behalf of Yad Vashem, the Holocaust Memorial in Jerusalem, I
intend to award Medals and Certificates of "Righteous among Nations" to
several Slovak citizens, under the auspices and in the presence of
H.E. Michal Kovac, President of the Republic of Slovakia, on 11 September
1997, at 14.00 hours, at the Primacialny Palac, Primacialne namestie 1,
Bratislava.

We shall be very glad and honoured to count with your presence at
this event and hope that you will be able to attend it. Kindly inform
directly the Presidential Protocol accordingly (Tel. 00-421-7-5317519).

This invitation includes your husband, Mr. Leonard Freedman, your
son Martin and your daughter Allison.

There should be no objection to videoing the ceremony for use on a
school education programme, but this should also be formally settled
with the President's Office.

Yours respectfully,

Yoel Sher
Ambassador of Israel

Mrs. Miriam Freedman
as Thanhago Avonue
London N3 3NA
UK

A-1180 Wien, Anton-Frank-Gasse 20 · Tel.: 470 47 41-45 · Fax: 470 47 46 *honour our rescuers Mrs. Helena Gavalovicova, Mrs. Maria Pernikova and many other dignitaries.*

As you can imagine, many painful memories have been evoked today, by being here in my birthplace of Bratislava. I have been back four or five times during my life, but none of these visits has meant as much to me as this one.

I do have a few happy childhood memories of being with my parents, my brother, sisters and my Slovakian friends, but sadly most of my memories are painful and tragic.

Speaking on behalf of my sister Zehava and myself, we are very grateful to be here today to personally thank Helena and Maria for what they and their husbands did for us. Thank you from the bottom of our hearts. These two people have proved that good can overcome evil. My two other sisters, Tova Glaser and Barbara Klein are with us today together with some of our children, and it is a miracle that we are here together.

Of course it was not in Bratislava, but in Nitra that the events I am referring to occurred. Helena and Maria and their husbands took upon themselves the dangerous and seemingly impossible task of rescuing and looking after my family.

The plan had originally been to rescue my uncle and aunt. That in itself would have been a great act of courage, but in the end they agreed to take eight members of the family into hiding. The group consisted of my mother, my sister Zehava and myself, together with my uncle and aunt and her two sisters and my cousin. We were hidden by these wonderful people in some flats, which were also occupied by members of the Gestapo. Can you imagine the risks they took to keep us nourished and to make sure that the "house guests" never met.

Because of their selfless and brave actions they placed themselves in a perilous situation. They risked their lives to save ours.

Mr Gavalovic and Mr Pernikov risked their lives every single day by caring for us as best they could, while Maria and Helena fed us and kept up our morale. Because of their dedication and devotion to our family these two young women sacrificed their own family life.

There are no words to express our gratitude to them all. Mr Gavalovic and Mr Pernikov have sadly passed away, but their spirits will live in all our hearts forever.

We will always cherish the memory of these wonderful people. Thank God that in those dark times a few loving caring and selfless individuals emerged, who were willing to risk their lives and put other people's lives before their own.

At that time Slovakia was swept into the madness of war. Man forgot God, forgot love and compassion. Dark clouds covered the country for several years.

But for Helena and Maria and their husbands, my family and I would not be here today.

We owe you everything. Thank you.

I was also contacted by The British Library and The Imperial War Museum where they displayed a commemorative family plaque.

Miriam with Prime Minister, David Cameron at a holocaust survivors convention at 10 Downing Street

RESCUE IN SLOVAKIA

The Prny family and Helena and William Gavalovic saved a family of eight Jews in Nitra, Slovakia, from deportation to Auschwitz. Miklos Fisher, who worked with Gavalovic, arranged for himself, his wife, her sisters and their children to hide in an empty bedsit in the block where Prny was caretaker. Despite the fact that part of the building was occupied by German soldiers, the Gavalovic and Prnys took turns bringing food and collecting laundry for those in hiding. In times of danger they were taken to a hidden cubby-hole in the cellar where there was only room to lie squeezed together, sometimes for as long as three days at a time.

In this way, three members of the Mannheimer family, two from the Weiss family, Seren Paskus and Miklos and Ela Fisher were saved.

Above from top: The Prny family

Helena and William Gavalovic

Miklos Fisher, his wife Ela with nephew Robi

Seren Paskus and Lily

Above from top: Solomon and Olga Mannheimer. Solomon became separated from his family during a round-up and was later murdered.

Their daughters Eva, Noemi and Edith Mannheimer. Eva was hidden, but Noemi perished. Edith was deported to a concentration camp, but survived.

Their son, Marci Mannheimer, who died in Mauthausen or Ebensee.

Olga and her daughters Gerty, Edith and Eva. Gerty had also been in hiding with her mother and Eva.

CHAPTER SEVEN

Meeting Irina Tweedie

"In the whole of the universe there are only Two: The Lover and The Beloved. God loves his Creation, and the Soul loves God. In order to be able to create, the One Being had to become two, and Logically there had to be a difference between the two. The creation was only possible because of the two opposites. Everything in creation responds either to the positive

*or the negative forces, or vibrations. There is the Sound or the
Echo, the Call and the response to it, Light or the Darkness.
Without the opposing forces, how could the world exist?"*

Daughter of Fire (pp. 180-81), Irina Tweedie

Opening the Heart

IN THE BEGINNING I felt very alone in my quest for spiritual enlightenment. To the outside world I was a wife, a mother and a Yoga teacher. But a new secret life was starting to unfold within me. As long as I continued to fulfill the expectations people placed in me in my everyday life, I felt free to continue searching for esoteric knowledge.

During the 1960s and 70s there was a tremendous explosion of spiritual groups in London. Some were very exclusive and required that potential members pass through a vetting procedure before being accepted. The starting point on my spiritual journey had been my love of Yoga—a discipline which became a way of life and helped to heal my body. It also awakened a need in me to experience the source of wisdom that lay within the practices. I instinctively felt that I would know my path when I found it—and, with Lennie's help, began to investigate some of the spiritual groups that were emerging.

In 1979 I fell into an emotional and physical decline. I had no energy and lost interest in everything, encountering a terrible emptiness, which I longed to fill with some kind of peace. I was about to encounter the light of my life, and my spiritual life was about to flower, and the real adventure was set to begin.

There was a period when a lot of people came to the West to teach Yoga. When Sri Vishnudevananda came for a time to London, I realised that I must carry on teaching. I was teaching physical Hatha Yoga and I was doing some meditation, but I was not yet involved with any deep techniques. I used to have pupils coming once a week and that was brilliant for me because I could experiment and truly start to learn what Yoga was all about.

I made some enquiries at Barnet College about teaching there. I met the head of the Sports Department who said, "We're looking for a Yoga teacher for the college and I wonder if you'd like to teach for us?" I had my qualification so I replied, "Yes I'll try it." We got on very well and he gave me many classes to teach. They were big classes with as many as forty or fifty people attending. At that time in the 1970s Yoga was very popular. I was surrounded by students but had

*A Yoga class at
The Cheshire Hall
in Hendon, 1973*

no personal relationships with them. I decided that I would like to understand my students on a deeper level. I studied the Doctor Schultz method of Autogenic Training with Velta Wilson. It was a form of relaxation therapy and meditation, which I was able to integrate into my work. I held group classes for a two-month period in my home. I really enjoyed this work.

I got into Yoga initially for just one purpose: to heal myself. My Yoga teacher told me that things would get worse before they improved. I enjoyed the postures tremendously because I had always been keen on sport. At the boarding school I ran, swam and was brilliant at handball. I took part in many competitions.

I was practising Yoga with an Israeli friend of mine who knew I was looking for a meditation teacher. She had heard of a Russian lady in North London who was holding meditation meetings in her home. Her name was Mrs. Irina Tweedie.

I watched a television documentary in a series about the spiritual path called *The Light of Experience* where every week they interviewed unusual people like Ravi Shankar, Krishna Murti, Swami Bhavyananda and other great teachers. Lennie thought I was giving far too much attention to Indian teachers and said, "There's a Russian lady on television tonight.... You should watch her." The documentary was about a female mystic called Irina Tweedie. Most of my previous teachers were Indian. She was Russian.

The programme was broadcast late in the evening, but we managed to see it. Mrs. Tweedie told the interviewer about meeting her guru and that he had asked her to keep a diary. The idea was that the diary would become a book, which would inspire, inform and help many people along the spiritual path.

While I watched, something happened to me that had never happened before. All I could see were Mrs. Tweedie's eyes—two blue eyes that were like an ocean of love. I might have fainted or been transported inside my mind because for a while I didn't understand what she was saying. When the programme finished, I turned to Lennie and said, "This woman's completely different from all the other teachers I've met."

In the documentary Mrs. Tweedie explained that her teacher belonged to a Sufi path and that the central core of Sufi teachings is the human heart. The Sufi path revolves around the heart. The heart is at the centre of the divine mystery and the Sufi quest. It is hidden where the mystical journey takes place. The Sufis believe that there is a substance in the heart which does not belong to the physical world.

Mrs. Tweedie belonged to a non-denominational order of Sufis who intended that the teachings should be available to all seekers of all religions. She said that Sufism and Yoga are one and the same. They are just words. In wisdom there are no differences. She said, "The roads to God are as many as there are human beings on earth." She made the point that Sufis don't convert anybody and that the truth can be found in every religion.

I rang my friend. I told her about my out-of-body experience while I was watching the documentary and she said, "Miriam, I've got her address." Mrs. Tweedie had no telephone so her number and her address were not listed anywhere. She didn't want people to know how to contact her. She only gave her address to people she wanted to see.

My friend, who had also watched the TV programme, heard that Mrs. Tweedie held a meditation meeting on Friday nights. We went there together, but initially we couldn't find the right building. She lived in a flat, but it was in a big house. We went to the main entrance and rang the bell, but got no answer. We were about to give up when a woman on a bicycle arrived and we asked her if she knew Mrs. Tweedie and she replied, "Yes, I do and I'm going to see her now." It was three days after I had seen her on the TV programme. We went in and saw assembled a group of people: some were seated, some sat on the floor, some sat with their backs to the wall while yet others lay on the floor. It was a disappointment. I had dreamt of sitting cross-legged in front of a guru, who would discourse and give instruction. My experiences at Yoga centres in the UK had conditioned me to expect this. I assumed it would be like that, but it wasn't— far from it! To start with, I couldn't see her anywhere in the flat. Eventually I caught sight of her cooking in the kitchen. A short time later she came into the room. She was not at all what I had expected.

We told her that it had been difficult to find the flat and that we were both Yoga teachers. I tried to engage with her, but she didn't talk to me, choosing only to address my friend. She told her that she held two meditation sessions on Fridays—one early and one later in the evening. She said that we could attend either session. I responded gratefully and said, "Thank you very much, but I can't stay. It's Friday night, our Sabbath, and I have to make a dinner for my family," and left. Shortly after this I went to Israel to visit my mother and didn't think about the meeting. When I returned to the UK, a friend told me that Mrs. Tweedie always asked where I was. She said that Mrs. Tweedie wanted to see me. This was very significant for me because at this time I did not have a full understanding of what was going on. I had not understood then that the disciple does not find the teacher, but that the teacher finds the disciple. This is the way it works. There is a saying that "When you are ready, the teacher appears." The teacher finds the pupil. But I didn't want to see her again. I didn't feel pulled towards her.

My friend said, "Come on, give Mrs. Tweedie a chance. She's asking for you. She's a very great lady." I don't know what it was she saw in me, but she must have seen something. So I decided to go and to learn meditation from her. Previously I was sitting in front of a Yoga guru in the crossed-legged position, but I found this very hard and nearly gave up. On my first visit to Mrs. Tweedie she told me to be in any position that was comfortable so that my body would not ache and distract me from the meditation. When I next visited Mrs. Tweedie, things had started to improve between us. On my third visit her eyes held me strongly. There was so much energy and charisma. I started to realize more and more that there was something very special about this woman. I felt I must give the relationship a chance to flower.

She graced me with a dream experience and it was this: I saw a bungalow with four chimneys. People were coming and going and there was some sort of commotion going on in the centre of this house. I was invited to come in. In terms of Sufi teaching the four chimneys

Irina Tweedie in Miriam's group. Miriam is seated on her right.

were highly significant. Mrs. Tweedie said these were spiritual symbols. She didn't say anything more.

When I told Mrs. Tweedie about the dream, she responded with, "Darling, you really will fit in very well. Why don't you come regularly? We meet here every day at this time. Otherwise whenever you've got time, do please come."

I was hooked. I was "branded." At first it was a very personal relationship, but I had little knowledge of her teachings really. The atmosphere was remarkably informal and relaxed, even though everyone addressed her as Mrs. Tweedie.

Her teachings encouraged us to *be*, to find ourselves, to be fully realized. This was her only goal and she

never deviated from it. Initially I found this very difficult to understand. She didn't lecture. Anything could
happen. It wasn't an ashram, it was a spiritual home.
Mrs. Tweedie didn't charge for her spiritual teaching
and training. She gave it freely. If she wanted to travel,
she would close the centre, and if she considered that
someone did not fit into the group, she was fully prepared to ask them to leave.

She taught a Sufi meditation practice, which starts
from the heart *chakra*. The most important thing she
gave us was love. It was a very powerful message. We
saw her as a bridge from the mundane to the divine. We
all fell in love with her.

She would say, "This path is only for the few. There
are no disciples. We are free, but we must discipline
ourselves and learn to stand alone.

"Some of the people who come here have been with
me for a long time. They are the nucleus. Some just

*Irina Tweedie, Agnes Kunze
(Head of the Leper Colony)
and Miriam*

come for one or two years and they go elsewhere. It is not for everyone."

I never knew what would happen when I visited Mrs. Tweedie. I began to meditate at home and I went to her regularly—every day in fact. I couldn't keep away. Lennie was very tolerant about me going to visit her so much. He may have thought that she represented my mother. It's difficult to explain what happened there. Sometimes she talked, sometimes she meditated, and at times she went into the garden or the kitchen. We didn't know what was expected of us.

I was learning about myself through what I projected onto my teacher and what she reflected back to me. If I went to her in a good mood, I would return home in a bad mood. If I visited her in a bad mood, she would completely ignore me. I didn't know what she expected from me, but it was an adventure and it still fascinates me to this day. She had such a unique and unpredictable method of teaching. I know it was a special privilege to be with her—just to sit and observe her interactions with people. Sometimes she was human and down to earth, and at other times she seemed divine. Sometimes she was full of love and compassion, and at other times she was angry and harsh. I suppose we all received the same benefits and did not want to force things. She gave us what we needed.

"Listening to the inner voice," she explained, "is what we learn to do here. We learn to recognise and then learn to listen to that inner voice. When we know the inner voice, it becomes our guru. If you have a mystical experience, do not try to describe it. You will destroy it. It is difficult to reconcile these experiences with the

This is part of a thirty-foot mural by Angie Sillars in Ibiza.
Irina Tweedie is seated on the extreme right.
Miriam is sitting next to her.

world around us, but it is all one and the same. Our attitude changes, though outwardly we remain the same."

Maybe I was like a ripe fruit, ready for some experience that I had never had. I had suffered a lot in my life and perhaps I was going to have a very big experience in order to come to terms with my past. Sometimes she was furious with me and threw me out. "I am not a teacher," she would tell me. "I am not a guide. This is my home and I have no disciples. I let people in and if necessary I kick them out. I do nothing. I merely create the atmosphere here. Everything else is done for me. When people try to put me on a pedestal, I behave badly and I can behave very badly. I can swear in English as well as in Russian."

Mrs. Tweedie's charismatic personality had a very powerful effect on most people who met her. I know I wasn't alone in feeling like this. I have no doubt that

I projected onto her all of my hopes and longings and that this was central to the relationship. I adored her and I know that during my time with her I received exactly what I needed—no more, no less. She reflected back to me, magnified a hundred times, love, compassion and acceptance.

She used to say, "We meet in the night to experience the connection in silence. God is with us in silence." For me now, I feel I am closer to people when I am not with them, particularly in the silence of the night. We had to meditate regularly, *stilling the mind in the heart*. She said to me, "Think of someone you love and feel the love for them, and let the feeling of love be in your heart. If your mind continues to think, drown the thoughts in the feeling of love." The whole teaching was very subtle. She told us that "You have to pick up the thread. If you don't pick up the thread, you won't understand what I'm doing."

It was a very deep and intense relationship. She taught us how to meet the silence and how to find our-

Miriam,
Irina Tweedie,
Hanka and
Mrs. Galloway

selves. I did have a tremendous number of experiences and entered a state of super-consciousness experiencing many psychic, spiritual dreams.

The intensity of my "experience explosion" stemmed from the fact that my *kundalini* energy had been activated and released. This is how Gopi Krishna describes the *kundalini* energy: "*Kundalini* is an unconscious, instinctive or libidinal force. *Kundalini* is described in certain Yoga *Upanishads* as lying 'coiled' at the base of the spine. It is also envisioned as either a goddess or a sleeping serpent. A *kundalini* awakening can occur in deep meditation and produce enlightenment and bliss. In practical terms, one of the most commonly reported *kundalini* experiences is the feeling of a burning electric current running along the spine." I tuned into Mrs. Tweedie's energy.

The Sufi system is not like ordinary Yoga. It starts from the heart *chakra*. When the heart *chakra* is activated, the two halves—the divine and the physical halves—come together and a very powerful energy is released. Once this heart *chakra* is opened, the other centres also open up.

I was not fully aware of what she was doing but I trusted her. I knew that her path was one of divine love and that it suited me. Her goal was to open up the love within us. Many of us did not fully appreciate or understand what she was doing and this included me. We fell in love with her because she was so extraordinarily beautiful and intelligent. She was very caring as well. She helped me in every aspect of my life. We all thought she was a divine woman because she could open the heart *chakra* in us.

She was using Yoga in a different way. I had a meditation *mantra*, which was given to me by Swami Vishnudevananda. He was a very stern man or so he seemed to me. He gave me a name when he initiated me: *Sarasvati*, which is the name of a poetess. He told me, "This is the name I want you to have, but if you forget it, you can use *Om*." I told him that I would never forget the name.

Mrs. Tweedie also gave me another *mantra*. She worked on another level. I told her that I wanted to learn how to meditate her way and she said, "Just sit still. Empty your heart. Think about the Divine." In our meditation we go deep into ourselves—deeper and deeper into our own most hidden place, our true self. The goal was that we should aim to go into our innermost being, into the core of ourselves, to find a place where there is peace, stillness and above all love.

"God is love," say the Sufis. Human beings are all love for they are made in His image. The problem is that we forgot this a long time ago. When we love another human being, however deeply, there is a place in our heart where this beloved human being has no access. There we are quite alone, but within us there is a longing, which is an ultimate proof that this place is reserved for Him alone. When we have found this place, we must imagine that we are seated there, immersed in and surrounded by the love of God. We are in deepest peace. We are loved. We are sheltered. We are secure. Our whole being is there. The physical body—everything. Nothing is outside, not even a fingertip, not even the tiniest hair. Our whole being is contained within the love of God. As we sit there happy and serene in his presence, thoughts will intrude into our mind—what we did the day before, what we have to do tomorrow, and so on. Memories flow and images appear before the mind's eye. We have to imagine that we are getting hold of every thought, every image and feeling, and then we drown them. We merge them into the feeling of love.

Every feeling, especially the feeling of love, is much more dynamic than the thinking process. So if one does it well, with utmost concentration, all thoughts will disappear. Nothing will remain. The mind will be empty. This is our meditation. It is a spiritual practice to control the mind. It requires will power. After a while when we practise it well, we will not fail to notice that this place in the heart and a higher state of consciousness are one and the same. This is the spiritual clarity we seek. It is a state that is beyond the mind. The mind can only understand what is outside itself. In other words, "I'm here and this *is* the knowledge." It is a higher state of consciousness known as *Samadhi*. We are the knowledge. There's no other reality to understand and you are one. In fact this state is indescribable in words.

The repetition of the *mantra* is the method we use. As Mrs. Tweedie used to tell us, "When you say a hundred times Coca-Cola, you don't become Coca-Cola, but you will understand the concept of what it is." We use a *mantra* that inspires us. Inspiration is very important. It is *the* important thing.

Mrs. Tweedie did not like to be considered a teacher. She described herself as "the caretaker of the flat," nothing more. Her flat was small with very little furniture— a bed, just a few cushions and some blankets and these were given to her by some of her students. She lived very simply and she paid her way with her state pension and the small pension left to her by her husband, who had been a naval officer.

Her door was always open to visitors from two until six in the afternoon and she gave her time freely. Some years later, when too many people were crowding in her hall, unable to sit down, she imposed more restrictions, but her door was never closed to those who needed her. She was very generous with her time. She adored cats, but she lived alone. She loved to work in her garden and it was very beautiful. In fact it was magnificent. I often took her to garden centres to buy plants and from time to time we went out shopping together.

Mrs. Tweedie wanted to experience one of our festivals and one evening at Passover she came to our ceremony and then we served her supper. She wanted to participate in our Jewish festival and I didn't know what she would eat. I made traditional chicken soup with roast chicken for the family. She ate this food for the same reason even though she was vegetarian. She said, "You invited me, and you cooked a meal for me and your family, and I respect what you've done."

I found this attitude amazing and inspiring. Mrs. Tweedie was a vegetarian after meeting her master, who was known as Guruji. His full name was Mahatma Radha Mohan Lal Ji. He once said to her, "Do not turn anything into a religion. You can turn vegetarianism into a religion. I must not eat this, I must not eat that. Don't be too extreme in anything."

I was also mostly a vegetarian long before I met Mrs. Tweedie through my studies and my practice of Hatha Yoga.

I learned a lot about respect and tolerance even though there were many difficulties between Mrs. Tweedie and myself. It may have been as a result of my personality. At times I found her very masculine and at other times, very feminine: sometimes hard and sometimes soft. She had a remarkable and inspiring quality. She could be harsh and then very warm. At the beginning I didn't treat her as a guru. I treated her like a friend, which was wrong. I misunderstood the basis of our relationship from the outset. It seemed she sought to draw me to her and then she expected me to realize that she was never going to be all those things for me that I wanted her to be. The correct relationship to her would be that of student to teacher. Her teaching was very subtle.

At first Mrs. Tweedie told me she could contact Guruji, her teacher, at any time she wanted. She told me it had happened after his passing when she was in the Himalayas at the Ghandiji ashram. She had the experience in deep meditation of Guruji merging with her. Since that time she just had to call him and Guruji was there. She could talk to him and had contact with him on another and higher plane of consciousness.

I discovered that I also had contact with her teacher. From then on at night Guruji would come to me and give me many experiences, which I recorded in my diary following Mrs. Tweedie's request. Every time I went to her she would ask me, "Did you have contact last night?" And I would tell her how real it was for me.

I was meditating one night and Lennie was snoring. Guruji was sitting on my bed and I said, "Guruji, I can't meditate when Lennie is snoring." Instantly he stopped snoring and I was amazed. On another occasion when I was meditating, I heard a choir singing beautifully in my room. When I told Mrs. Tweedie about this experience, she said she had had the same experience and that I was tuning into the celestial sound.

My connection to Guruji grew stronger. I felt that Mrs. Tweedie couldn't accept that an ordinary person like me could have these experiences. I was totally amazed that I was having them. Maybe it was a test for both of us.

This was nonetheless the start of an intense relationship, which lasted until her death and has continued to this day for me on the spiritual level. The relationship between the teacher and the student is like a marriage and there can never be a divorce!

She didn't ask about my past, my childhood, my suffering and the loss of my loved ones. I believe that she knew intuitively what I had been through. She just said, "You came here to find yourself and you will find yourself."

I really wanted to find myself and she knew that. I had to overcome my painful memories and this was difficult for me.

I knew that people would find it hard to understand my training and what the relationship was between pupil and teacher. I was completely open to Mrs. Tweedie and it turned my life upside down. I understood that she did things differently from other teachers. Her guru made her look at the darkness within herself and she did this in the same way with me. I had to find myself, to ask, "Why am I here? What am I?" I was fearful, but I had a deep longing and knew something was missing in my life. Mrs. Tweedie nurtured this longing in me.

This longing for truth was immensely powerful—so powerful that I couldn't explain it. I just wanted to be like her, although I had put her on a pedestal. I thought she was much more than human and that was why she was starting to treat me very badly. She wanted me to realize that she was just a human being. She may have had some higher attributes but I treated her like a superhuman. This was a very big mistake on my part. When you love somebody and trust them so much, it can blind you to what is truly going on.

At the beginning I was very outspoken with her and should have known better. I wanted to be her friend and to be close to her. In fact, I wanted to be her favourite. It was madness and selfish on my part. In the Sufi tradition, when you are with a teacher, you don't talk first. The teacher has first to talk to you. When you go to the Queen, you do not talk to the Queen, she approaches you. Mrs. Tweedie was my teacher and I was not supposed to talk to her unless she talked to me. That is the ancient teaching tradition and that's the way it is.

If she asked me something, then I could answer her, but I should not have come forward and forced myself on her to gain her attention. It wasn't acceptable behaviour; it was bad manners and I could not see this or I chose not to. I didn't understand how these things worked. In the beginning she let it be. But gradually she wanted me to understand. She threw some people out of the group when they misunderstood her and I watched this happening. It made me hysterical and I wondered what they could have done to deserve this kind of treatment, never realizing that later it was going to happen to me too. "Get out. Get out," she exclaimed. When I first saw this happen, I nearly had a heart attack, but she had her reasons. I think she did it to help us see ourselves more clearly. We had to look deep into ourselves. Why did I get so upset when she told somebody off? I would sit there and she'd say, "I speak to the wall when I'm speaking to the door." I had to understand this very subtle way of teaching. I was learning to grasp the thread of what she was doing and it fascinated me.

I went to see her regularly, even though I was teaching every day and had a lot of family responsibilities. My visits to Mrs. Tweedie became very important in my life and I was there nearly every day sometimes until eleven o'clock at night. I would go home to make dinner for my family and then return to sit with her. I used to cook and shop for her as well if she asked me to; it was a pleasure for me and effortless as I was serving my teacher. I sought to do what was expected of me and, because I was spending so much time with her she said, "Tell your family you are just looking after an old lady." In truth she was looking after me! Besides my family she became the main force in my life.

She gave us very little direct instruction and I found that difficult as I expected information on the teaching. She would talk about anything from the Himalayas to being in the north of Scotland, cooking, gardening, families and her teacher. We would drink tea together and sometimes she made a meal. She transmitted love and created a feeling of togetherness, and she changed people's lives.

Even so I was feeling something of an outsider as I had my family and did not mix socially with the other people in the meditation group. I watched as people became more and more friendly with each other. When she gave others her attention, I could become very jealous. I wanted her to be mine and mine alone. Our relationship was not good all the time. I didn't understand that I had to share her with everyone in the group. I found this extremely hard to accept so I had to learn the hard way.

The trouble was that I was absorbed in her personality first and not in the teaching. She was so charismatic. There were many people there who were going through exactly the same process, but she treated me differently. It never occurred to me that the others could be jealous of me. I can see now that may have been difficult for them.

One day she announced, "I'm closing at three o'clock today and I'm going out with Miriam." And we would go out together—just the two of us—shopping, to a park, to Kew Gardens, to Kenwood House, and often she would come to my home. I never asked her why she would close the meeting and come out with me, because I loved to go out with her and didn't care what anyone else thought. I never queried her methods; she had her reasons and I didn't understand the purpose behind them. The problem was that, when she did this, it caused jealousy among the other people in the group and they wondered why I was being treated differently, why I was getting so much of her attention. I can understand now that she behaved in this way towards me not because she especially liked me but because she wanted to teach me and the others a lesson. That was one of her methods of teaching.

She came to my house on a number of occasions because at that time I was having big problems with my *kundalini* energy. When it occurred, it was frightening—I did not know what was happening. I had pain in my whole body—a burning sensation all over. I knew from Yoga books about the "serpent power," but never dreamt it would happen to me. It was unexpected and a great surprise. What I understood from Yoga books is that it is essential to go slowly and gently. When one practices Yoga, *pranayama*, meditation with the grace of God and of the guru, it happens. "My God!" I exclaimed. "What is happening to me?" It was like a volcanic explosion of energy and it frightened me. It caused havoc in my whole body and mind. "What am I going to do? Who is going to help me?"

I ran to Mrs. Tweedie to tell her and blame her for the situation. She said, "Darling, don't worry. I will help you. I will support you." But it was not all right. I had more and more trouble, pain, suffocation, emptiness, nothingness, fear. I was losing my mind. Ancient writings say that *Kundalini* is the Queen of the nervous system, controlling the thousands of *Nadis, Idas,* and *Pingale* and *Shushumna* (linked to the nervous system) of the body. Without them the body cannot exist.

Mrs. Tweedie knew at that time she needed to support me and hold me. Then one day she turned to me and said, "I cannot treat you with kid gloves forever. You will have to stand on your own feet." For some time I didn't understand what she meant. She had held me and supported me and gave me whatever I needed at the time, but when I demanded more, she would become harsh and angry. When many people came to her home, she hugged them and gave them lots of attention but completely ignored me. She did this intentionally. Whatever she did she had a clear purpose in her mind.

When she was nice to others, it caused me pain. It was such a harsh type of teaching and we were expected to understand. I am not sure if this was the normal approach to teaching Sufism, but I knew Guruji had treated Mrs. Tweedie harshly. With Mrs. Tweedie there did not seem to be a structure in her method. The focus was on us and we had to work on ourselves.

She came to my Yoga classes, no doubt to see how I taught. She watched me carefully. She also took part in the *Yoga Nidra* guided visualisation sessions I ran. She sent many of her group to my classes.

On one occasion she went to the kitchen and made tea, which she served with cake. But she gave me nothing. She took some cake for herself and gave some to the others, but gave nothing to me. I sat and watched while this happened and wondered what was going on. I burst into tears and she asked me, "Oh darling, why are you crying? What is bothering you?" She played with me like a cat plays with a mouse. She wanted to see if I was jealous. There were many other incidents like this. She must have thought carefully about her relationship with me, but she never explained what was going on. She never attempted to make her method clear to me. She left me hanging. It was painful and deeply confusing. I see now that she was dealing with my ego, that had become inflated after having received so much of her attention. That was part of her method and she tested people all the time.

One Christmas she invited me to join her and some other people from the group to celebrate, but when I arrived she said, "I never called you! What made you come?" She really gave me the shock treatment. I wanted the ground to open up so I could disappear. I was very hurt by these things and that's just what she didn't want to happen. She didn't aim to hurt me. She wanted me to understand what was really happening. She could change her mind instantly.

She often did some very strange things, which were very difficult for me to grasp. The first time when she threw me out for something I did, she just said, "Go!" I knew that traditionally when a teacher throws you out, that after this happens three times, they have to accept the disciple. I knew this was special and that she didn't do this to all the people in the group. She never said to them, "Go on, get lost. I never want to see you again." She didn't want other people in the group to talk to me when she'd thrown me out. She was testing me. She did this relentlessly and she never eased up or changed her method. I was able to cope with it. She told me often that she didn't treat her other followers like this. Like her I must have had a very strong personality and she tried to break it.

I did slowly start to understand that I was too attached and dependent on her. The Sufi path is about *non-attachment* and certainly not about dependence and jealousy. I had to break through these things to get to God. It was shock treatment, because selfish attitudes are of no use to the disciple. Her method was to achieve this through making me understand the hard way. It was very difficult.

Sometimes I stayed away for as long as a month, which was very hard on me and I suffered. When I crawled back to her, she didn't keep her door closed to me. She accepted me, but watched me carefully to gauge my reactions. I was beginning to understand what she was doing. I was changing. I was quieter in the group. I understood not to oppose, not to demand,

and that was what she wanted. I had to learn to be one of the group and that I was not someone special. She told me what she thought I needed to know.

I did many things for her. I did whatever she expected. Sometimes she closed the flat for many months while she travelled to India and to other destinations. When the full version of her diary was published as *Daughter of Fire*, she began to give lectures in Germany, the United States, Holland and Switzerland. I organised some of these trips for her. I travelled with her and other members of the group on some of these lecture tours and I held workshops and Yoga seminars on some of these trips. Sometimes there were as many as twenty or thirty of us travelling with her. I enjoyed these journeys abroad with her very much indeed. Mrs. Tweedie told me that, on a trip back from India whilst she was still with Guruji, she gave several talks at the Theosophical Society in London where she was a member. Guruji tested her ability to communicate her experiences to others. She then returned to India and stayed until Guruji died in 1967.

Whenever we travelled with her, she expected us to be well presented so that she would be proud of us. We always bought ourselves new clothes for these trips. When we met her at the airport, she often looked like a little old Russian peasant in a long skirt and a scarf. She could do this because we all looked so smart. She could do anything she liked. It was always a shock, but she did this purposefully. She did what she wanted because she was free and we were proud of her. We respected her and we were always most happy to go with her. She was just being herself and she wanted to teach us that appearances count for nothing. She was brilliant and she wanted to shock us, which she certainly did! She could read our minds.

She told us:

- We don't wear special clothes. They create a barrier between us and other people.

- Reading to gain knowledge is unnecessary; realise first, then read all you can about it.

- To experience one's self is the true knowledge.

- Watch out for the casual remark. It may be for you.

We went to a big transpersonal conference for a week in Davos in Switzerland. There were many important people there: The Dalai Lama, Marie-Louise von Franz, Stanislav Grof, Dr. Frederic Leboyer, Paul Horn,

Elsie, Margaret and Irina Tweedie

Gopi Krishna and even Albert Hoffman, the discoverer of LSD. It was very impressive.

At one point she took a group to the USA, but I couldn't go. It made her angry that I couldn't go with them all and I regretted afterwards not going.

In Davos and in Amsterdam I held meditation meetings and also gave a talk based on two poems written by Hannah Senesh, who was a heroine in the Second World War and was murdered by the Hungarian Gestapo. Several hundred people attended. It was a significant occasion and I was very pleased to be able to do this. I was serving Mrs. Tweedie and she helped me.

I was slowly starting to understand more about her method of teaching—learning to share—and our relationship was improving in leaps and bounds. But when I self-published a small book of my dreams called *Under the Mango Tree* (Astoria Publications, 1989), I don't think it met with her approval as she may have envisaged something rather different. Soon after I had met her, she had asked me to write down all my dreams, which I did, and she suggested I publish some of them. There were quite a number of dreams, as I was with her physically nearly every day for some seven years, and my dreams started within a few weeks of my first meeting her.

I was also featured in a Yoga magazine called *Yoga Today*. The editor of the journal came to one of my classes to interview me. Shortly after that I published my book, *Yoga at Work*. Mrs. Tweedie knew about this book and she did approve.

Mrs. Tweedie and I had very similar temperaments. She was a Russian and I am a Slav. We both had a tendency to let our anger explode. Sometimes her explosions were overwhelming and frightening. They would pass quickly and she would ask out of the blue, "Would you like a cup of tea? It's a lovely day today," as if absolutely nothing had happened. She could switch abruptly and take us all by surprise, but it was a pretence she adopted to shake us up. She wasn't really angry. She could switch abruptly. It was disconcerting.

Lennie was always most supportive of my interests and in the path I had chosen to follow, even though he took little interest in it himself. He liked Mrs. Tweedie and visited her with me. He never stood in my way or put up obstacles.

As I had studied *Patanjali* traditional Yoga with Indra Nash, in 1993 he asked me if I would like to travel to India with some other students. I desperately wanted to go and we went on a five-week tour to the ashrams of Sri Aurobindo, Ramana Maharshi, Swami Sivananda, Swami Chidananda Saraswati, Vivekananda and more.

I was invited by Indra Nash to attend a talk in Rishikesh by Swami Chidananda, whom I had met in London many years before. I listened to his talk, but it was in Hindi as it was at many of the sessions I attended. Even though I didn't understand the language, I was able to carry on with my meditation. Indra Nash said to me, "Look, there are many people here. Why don't you go to speak to him?" I didn't think it was going to work out, but I managed to get near to him and I said, "Swami Ji, I'm so honoured to meet you again and to see you." He knew who I was and I was most impressed that he recognised me after twenty years. We talked and it was a very profound experience.

On this journey I met a number of great spiritual teachers including Swami Gitananda. He had the most

Miriam in India

beautiful wife, Menaksha Devi, who was American but looked Indian. They had a son called Ananda.

I went to Kanpur to visit Guruji's centre and I was the guest of his youngest son, Satendra. Sitting in Guruji's home was an empowering and inspiring experience. I tuned into him. I was in the same place that Mrs. Tweedie had received her training.

While I was in Kanpur, I was always in touch with Lennie and he was fantastic. He wouldn't go to any of those places but he was very happy for me to go. I contacted him once a week and he knew I was with friends.

At this stage of my life I was still focusing on physical Hatha Yoga. I attended many seminars on meditation and the theory of the *chakras*, which focused on techniques for stilling the mind. But none of these seminars and teachers made a deep impression on me. I went to America with Lennie. I was learning to cope without seeing Mrs. Tweedie constantly. I could visualise that Mrs. Tweedie was a part of me and that I was a part of her. I was beginning to integrate her into my life in a very positive way. I no longer needed to be with her all the time and this was a big step forward for me. I was certainly making progress. She said to me, "If you are constantly with me, I cannot help you, and if you put me on a pedestal, I feel sure I cannot help you. You just have to accept me for what I am."

In 1999 I went to see Mrs. Tweedie shortly before she died. She was a very old lady and it all felt final. I realized that this was the last time I was going to see her. It is still hard for me to fully comprehend just how much she did for me. She completely transformed my outlook on life and she gave me confidence, hope and courage and made me stronger. She said to me once, "Guruji wants you to do his work. You've got a great gift with people and I want you to work with people."

And that is what has happened with my ongoing meditation groups. I am still working on integrating everything Mrs. Tweedie taught me, but my mission in life is clear to me. It is to pass on Mrs. Tweedie's and Guruji's teachings the best way I know. She used to say that "Travelling the path of love is like walking on a hair across a chasm of fire."

Very often I was the last one to understand what was truly going on. Life is certainly a mystery and often we do not realize how much we are changing. You can meditate, you can pray, you can serve humanity selflessly, but you just don't see it for yourself.

I try to work from heart to heart. I want to transmit love in the best way that I am able. Mrs. Tweedie opened my heart for which I am eternally grateful. She said to me once, "It's all done through your eyes and through your heart." And this is very, very true. I often just had to tell her how much we all loved her and she accepted this with grace and affection. She taught me so much but I'd be the first to admit that I still have much to learn to this day. She wanted me to achieve peace of mind, to accept life, and to surrender to the light within my heart.

Sometimes Mrs. Tweedie was very hard on me. Looking back I can see that she couldn't be hard on some people because of their constitution and lack of inner strength. She was treated very hard by her guru because she was a strong, healthy woman, but one who was attached to material and intellectual things. She wanted to be one with the truth that Guruji gave her. She *"wanted truth like a drowning man needs air."*

She could see that I was very strongly attached to my children. As Kahlil Gibran wrote in *The Prophet,* "Our children are not our possessions." They come from us, but they are not ours. We cannot control their minds. They have minds of their own and we must give them room to flower. That is just the way it is. Our children need our love. Everybody in this world needs love. We can care for our children—and we must—but we cannot control them. In truth the love that we seek is inside ourselves. We have to allow for space in our relationships. We must not cling to those we love. This was the gist of Mrs. Tweedie's teachings.

We can care for our children but we cannot possibly know what they are thinking. We all need our own space in which to grow and flourish. We are individuals and must give our loved ones our love without demanding anything in return. We must find that powerful love in our own hearts before we can share it. It is impossible to give something which you haven't found in yourself. This again is what I learned from Mrs. Tweedie.

She had a very deep understanding of these things. We want to be with people *and* to meditate. Time is very valuable; we can steal another's time just as we can steal their possessions, but we must not steal anything. Mrs. Tweedie had strict ethics about possessions. She said, "If you have two chairs and you need only one, it is stealing." She encouraged us to become unattached to material things, saying, "You can have beautiful things, but don't be attached."

Before she passed on, Mrs. Tweedie nominated Llewellyn Vaughan-Lee as her successor. He is English and is domiciled in America now. Before he went to America, he had invited Mrs. Tweedie to move from her council flat to the ground floor flat in his house. She

Llewellyn, Miriam and Lennie

trained Llewellyn so that he could take over from her and she trained other people to do her work in different ways. In 1991, Llewellyn moved to Northern California and founded The Golden Sufi Centre to help make available the teachings of this Sufi lineage. He currently lives in California and is the author of many books on Sufism and Spiritual Ecology.

My knowledge of Sufism is actually very limited. There is a vast amount of literature on the subject. Idris Shah opened the door to many with his translations and helped spread the teachings throughout the world. As far as I am concerned, it is a path of love, friendship, sharing and giving.

The Sufi path of Mrs. Tweedie's teacher was known as *Naqshbandiyya Mujaddidiyya*. Guruji's teacher, who was called Guru Maharaji, described Sufism as not being a religion. Mrs. Tweedie was the first woman to bring this teaching to the West and she trained us in the old, traditional way. She always talked openly about Guruji. She called him "Bhai Sahib," which means "elder brother."

CHAPTER EIGHT

Dreams and Reflections

"We are people of peace. We unite. We do not divide. Guruji's life was devoted to the single objective of uniting hearts. All of us who continue his work do the same. It sounds easy, but uniting hearts is the most difficult thing in the world."

Irina Tweedie

Irina Tweedie and Miriam

SOON AFTER I MET MRS. TWEEDIE, my dreams took on a new intensity. They were visionary and lucid dreams. I entered a higher state of consciousness. Mrs. Tweedie was often in the dreams and was able to help me to interpret them. These dreams gave me insight into my innermost self and afforded me a deep understanding into the meaning and purpose of the creation. Many deep truths and insights into the spiritual path were revealed to me in my dreams.

Before my first year with Mrs. Tweedie had passed, her teacher, Guruji, contacted me and was appearing regularly in my dreams. She remarked that, when this started to happen, there were times when her contact with her guru was more difficult and she couldn't always reach him. This worried me and I wondered if it meant that in some way I was interfering with her work. Nonetheless the dreams continued and I went on sharing them with Mrs. Tweedie whenever she asked me to.

I dreamed profusely and I recorded them all, reflecting on their meaning. Some of the dreams were related to my relationship with Mrs. Tweedie and Guruji, whilst others seemed to be more collective in nature. On some occasions I had dreams that I was told were for or about other people.

During the time when the *kundalini* energy was activated in me, I dreamt many dreams of a dormant serpent in the base of my spine, being awakened. On an everyday and physical level, the experience was very painful, as I felt infused with a tremendous energy and my mind felt explosive. I felt a burning sensation throughout my body. When this happens, the mind struggles to understand what is taking place and to remain in charge. But this experience has nothing to do with the mind. Through the influence of Yoga, prayers, meditation and the grace of God, I was gradually able to contain the intensity of this energy.

Simultaneously my Hatha Yoga teaching improved enormously and the love for my pupils became tremendous. Everyone I met, in whatever situation, seemed to be a better human being, beautiful and different, and somehow a part of this field of love at the centre of my life. I began to realize that all of my *chakras* were being activated. I was again experiencing some unusual physical experiences with an aching throat that throbbed for weeks and hurt so much that I thought I might suffocate. But, throughout all of this discomfort, I continued to feel a great love for Mrs. Tweedie.

Gradually I began to feel an enormous happiness growing at the centre of my being. I wanted to shout it from the rooftops, "God is real!" There was no doubt about it for me any more, and nobody could take this realization away from me. I experienced a great bliss which lasted for many days. Members of my family commented on how radiant I was, as though I was in love.

One of the most important dreams I had happened shortly after I met Mrs. Tweedie and signified my finding of a true teacher. See section "Finding the teacher" in the next chapter.

In another dream, Guruji appeared as if he were on a cloud. He was dressed all in white and he was smiling. His face was as white as his clothes. His clothes remained white, but his face turned black.

I asked him, "What can I do for you?" In response he asked if I wanted to come to him.

"Yes," I replied, "but I want to stay here too."

Again I asked, "What can I do for you?"

He replied, "Cross the river."

I did and I found a wounded bird lying on the other side. When I tried to pick it up, it flew away.

"But how will I get back?" I asked.

"By train," came his response.

The train looked like a sleazy snake, with no windows or doors. It was terribly dark. I went inside it and told Guruji that I wanted to see light. "Open the window," he said. Immediately there was a window that I could open. I was hit by a powerful light and Guruji began to disappear. "Goodbye, old lady," he said. "How old am I?" I asked. "Ninety years old," he replied.

After this dream, I began to have some very strange and uncomfortable experiences. I felt as if a volcano was exploding inside me. It was complete inner chaos and I felt like a zombie. I understood later that these were experiences of the *kundalini* energy. I blamed all this on Mrs. Tweedie and I was furious that she was causing me so much trouble.

These experiences went on for many weeks. I didn't talk to anyone about it, not even my husband. I wondered why she was doing this to me. She always said, "I am not doing anything. It is done to us." I cursed her in my mind. I was frantic. I thought, "She has immense powers."

I knew Mrs. Tweedie didn't see anyone over the weekends, but everything got so bad that one Saturday morning I rushed over to her flat. On the way I had a strong feeling that she and I had become one. I felt I had taken over the pain that Mrs. Tweedie had experienced in India with Guruji. But when I got inside her flat, I said, "If this is your method of teaching the spiritual life, I won't come here anymore. I don't want to come here anymore."

Her response was, "Okay, don't come." But after a while I was begging her to help me. I knew that she was the only one who could help me. She said, "It will be done." After a few days I was fine. The longing in me grew and the love increased.

Mrs. Tweedie said, "A veil has been put around you and everything will become easier now." A very deep friendship began to flower.

Then I had this dream: Mrs. Tweedie came to me and her aura was in flame. She looked so calm and peaceful. I was trying to climb a ladder up a very tall building. Every time I went up three steps I stumbled back and it was like this for some time. People at the top of the building were shouting to me to come up. Finally I reached the top and immediately fell down to the bottom. All of a sudden a white dove appeared. It was Guruji. The dove pushed me up to the top of the building and I fell into a big hole. I thought the flame in the dream could have referred to the burning experiences I had in *kundalini.*

One night after this dream I started to hear Guruji talking to me in a quite ordinary way. The next day I said to myself, "This isn't possible. It must be my imagination or an illusion." I told Mrs. Tweedie about this dream when I next went to see her at her flat. She told me to ask Guruji some questions. While she was in the kitchen, I went into a deep meditation in which I asked these questions: "Are you real?" "Will I ever have peace of mind?" and "Can I experience God?" The answers came right away. To my first question, Guruji said,

"Work it out for yourself." To the second he said, "It is granted." And to the last question he responded with, "You've got it." I told Mrs. Tweedie what happened and she said, "That's just how he would talk."

That night, I had an excruciating headache. It felt as though my skull had been split in half. I couldn't even get up to take some aspirin. All of a sudden Guruji appeared. I challenged him to prove that he was real. "If you are real, please take my headache away." He kissed my forehead and the headache was gone. I just lay there in sheer amazement. I woke up the next morning overwhelmed by such a feeling of happiness that again I wanted to shout from the rooftops, "God is real. There's no doubt about it anymore." I was bursting with joy. Something real and undeniable had happened to me, something nobody could ever take away, and that joy stayed with me for many days.

Every evening, when I began my meditation, Guruji was there. Sometimes he was an actual physical presence like an extremely vivid dream. Sometimes he was an energy. In both cases his presence was equally compelling. I started to talk with him about myself and he always answered me. He told me he was always with me, always watching me and helping me, and that I should be at peace. And most of the time I was. One evening though, when I was meditating, Lennie began to snore. I found this distracting and I asked Guruji to intervene. Lennie started to breathe normally. It was a simple incident, but it was another proof that I was experiencing something that I can only describe as grace.

My *kundalini* condition flared up again. The energy centres in my body—the *chakras*—had been activated. I learned that the activation of the heart *chakra* is the first step towards opening all the *chakras*. The energy centre in my throat began to hurt and I thought I might suffocate. This lasted for weeks. Again I attributed my condition to Mrs. Tweedie. Nonetheless I continued to feel great love for her.

I was abruptly seized by a painful longing. My mind was a mass of confusion and I felt I was losing control of myself. I felt I was going mad. But I was totally fascinated at the same time because I knew that something very important was happening. In spite of my inner turmoil I was glowing. I felt enormous love for my students and everyone looked different. I had a very strong desire to help people. I told Mrs. Tweedie about this and she responded with this quote: "The time will come when our hair is loved off and our eyes are falling out, but these things don't matter. If we are real, we cannot be ugly" (from *The Velveteen Rabbit* by Margery Williams).

And she added this quotation, *"Give me freedom to fly without a shadow. Give me freedom to sing without an echo and to love without leaving traces."*

I spent a long, long time pondering on the meaning of these words. These lyrics from a Swahili song later became the motto for Mrs. Tweedie's group.

Mrs. Tweedie told me, "You will get your answer in your dreams." And how right she turned out to be! My dream life had already opened up a great deal, but much more was still ahead for me. I realized that these experiences are not the true goal of the spiritual life, but they are nonetheless most encouraging. I was truly fortunate to have this encouragement in all the aspects of my pursuit of inner peace. In my case my spiritual life has always centred around my dreams.

April 21st 1980 was Mrs. Tweedie's 73rd birthday. It hardly seemed possible that I had met her only four months before. I went to visit her in her flat and was able to spend several hours alone with her. It was during that visit that I told Mrs. Tweedie of a recent experience in meditation in which I tried to embrace her and found that she was hollow. She was very pleased with this dream and said, "Thank God. Now you understand at last." Then it hit me that her existence in a human form was merely a disguise. I told her that I was sure she had come here to train me and some others and, when that was over, she could depart at any time. I knew it sounded greedy, but I prayed to God to keep her well. I told her how much I wanted her to stay with me because she was my inspiration. She made no direct response to this. She just started to tell me stories about her life.

Soon after this I started having more problems with the *kundalini* energy. A pattern seemed to be forming, but I was never given enough rest between these bouts. However, looking after my family and teaching my Yoga students kept me grounded. Yet, if I had known how hard the spiritual life was going to be, I never would have taken the first step. But by this time I was so attracted by the whole process that I wouldn't have stopped it for anything.

One night I had a dream which embodied the turmoil I felt inside: I saw the face of a young man and his head was embedded in a wall. It turned into two horrible penguins, who were entangled like snakes in what must have been sexual writhing. It was ghastly. The penguins turned into two chickens and they too were entangled in the same hideous way. I woke up feeling totally drained both physically and mentally.

I told Mrs. Tweedie about my horrible dream. She told me that things would get better, but that didn't happen right away. I was having a terrible time getting my housework done. The memory of those penguins and chickens filled me with dread. Eventually I felt better. In fact I suddenly learned a new way to do my housework. I let Guruji do it for me! He did everything, including the shopping. I would ask, "Guruji, can you help me?" And in a flash an energy took over and everything was just done. All the effort was eliminated.

One night in a dream, Guruji asked me a riddle: "A chicken hatched two eggs. One egg was hatched a half a day before the other egg, which is older?" I tried to solve it but I couldn't. Guruji only laughed. Then I had another dream: I looked out into the sea and the sky and saw thousands of blue eyes staring at me. They were Mrs. Tweedie's eyes, and the sky and sea were covered with them. When I told this dream to Mrs. Tweedie, she laughed and said nothing.

I was not in the habit of attending Synagogue, but one day Mrs. Tweedie told me that she wanted to come to the Synagogue with me. I picked her up the next day and took her to my Synagogue. We sat together for two hours or so listening to the Rabbi and she held my hand the entire time. I had heard this Rabbi speak before, but never so inspiringly. I was crying and we were both very moved.

I had another dream: I was in a graveyard. Heads were emerging from under the gravestones and they were smiling at me. I felt very uncomfortable and I sat down on one of the stones. Then the full bodies came out and circled me. The bodies danced around me, singing, "You're one of us."

Mrs. Tweedie had this to say about the dream, "The little self has died. That is very good." By the "little self" she meant the ego. I knew that wasn't true, but perhaps some aspect of me had died.

This was followed by another bout of *kundalini* problems. I was afraid I would go crazy. I had started to read Mrs. Tweedie's book, *Chasm of Fire*, which was the diary of her spiritual training with Guruji, and I was finding it quite disturbing. She told me to stop reading it, or any other books for that matter, at least for the time being. I remember that she often used to say, "The cup has to be empty before it can be filled."

I then began to be able to see Mrs. Tweedie's aura. It wasn't always the same. Sometimes it was white, sometimes yellow and sometimes pink. But it was *so* pure and catching a glimpse of it inspired me deeply.

One Friday night in meditation at Mrs. Tweedie's house I saw masses of deformed souls coming toward me. She told me that she saw them too. She explained that the souls at a lower level are often attracted to spiritual groups and that I was not to worry about it. Another night, while I was meditating at home, I heard a choir of children singing the purest sound. Even when I came out of the meditation, I could still hear those celestial voices. Mrs. Tweedie told me that I had tuned into the *infinite sound* and she added that she had a very similar experience in the Himalayas.

On several occasions Mrs. Tweedie told me, "The first two years are the hardest. After that everything will become easier for you."

I was suffering a lot of physical pain. I had pains in my heart and throat and I couldn't breathe. My mind was not acting normally either. It was as if I was being "vacuumed." I was seriously worried about my state of mind and I felt lethargic. For the sake of my husband and my family I hoped that my personality was not going to change. I could accept the internal changes, but externally I wanted to remain jolly and bright. I really felt that Mrs. Tweedie was controlling me and my mind. I also realized that I was deeply fascinated by what was happening to me. I felt that this was truly an extraordinary path I was on. I remembered her telling me that on this path it was possible to realize God in just ten years.

I was going through a terrible state of confusion. So many questions were burning inside me. So one day I wrote them all down and brought them to Mrs. Tweedie. These were my questions:

1. Why do you open the heart *chakra* to all newcomers, without knowing them at all?

2. Why do people's eyes shine so brightly?

3. Why does everybody have to go through this physical/emotional ordeal?

4. There's no teaching here, no discipline...what's this all about?

5. How do you know that students are ready? Maybe they just come out of curiosity or just to learn something about meditation?

6. How do you know that students undergo experiences? You always seem to know without being told.

7. Do you give us dreams and visions ... and why?

8. Do you want your students to depend on you or can they be away from you for a long time and develop by themselves?

9. Why do you feed the group? (She used to serve fabulous meals for us. Sometimes to as many as four to six people every night and sometimes more).

10. You talk about longing all the time, but I don't have any longing ... except to be with you. What is this longing supposed to be about?

11. My mind is in a vacuum. My concentration and memory are hopeless. What's the purpose of all this?

12. I don't want to change externally, but people are noticing changes in me all the time. They tell me my eyes are shining, and ask me if I have a lover. Yes, I'd like to have peace of mind, but no more, please! Everybody here is so lethargic. Why?

13. I have a desire to understand many things. I want to help my Hatha Yoga students but I have some kind of intellectual need. My mind doesn't work well, so how can I help people? I want my mind to improve, but not to change.

14. It is supposed to be a loving group but in ways it seems to be quite the opposite. There are so many secrets. There doesn't seem to be any real camaraderie in the group. What is that all about?

Mrs. Tweedie never answered any of these questions. She thought they were stupid. She became very angry and stormed out into the garden. After a while, she came back in and offered me a cup of tea. She started talking about Tyaga, the path of renunciation, which she took, or more correctly, the path which was chosen for her. I couldn't understand why she was bringing it up. I had been feeling so sorry for myself, and I thought I wasn't even on that path. Perhaps she was trying to make me feel better by putting things in perspective. Apparently, everything could be quite a bit worse.

CHAPTER NINE

Dreamscapes

"The dream is a little hidden door in the innermost and most secret recesses of the soul, opening into that cosmic night which was the psyche long before there was any ego-consciousness, and which will remain psyche no matter how far our ego-consciousness extends.... All consciousness separates; but in dreams we put on the likeness of that more universal, truer, more external man dwelling in the darkness of primordial night. There is still the whole, and the whole is in him, indistinguishable from the nature and the bare of all egohood. It is from these all-uniting depths that the dream arises, but it never so childish, grotesque and immoral."

Carl Jung, "The meaning of psychology for modern man"
(Collected Works Vol. 10: *Civilisation in Translation*)

THESE DREAMS WERE GIVEN TO ME, and are personal. Yet they belong to all of you who can respond to them. I never remembered my dreams until I met my spiritual teacher. When I shared my dreams with her, I began to realise how great is the significance and power of the unconscious, and I become aware of the ineffable source of the dreams. This understanding came because she told me to write them down so they could help me in my spiritual growth and help others. I offer very little interpretation of the dreams, but I have decided to explain some of them in order to give some clues and pointers. But each person who reads them will find a meaning in their own way. I have found that when I re-read the dreams, they brought change to my life. I find new gifts of meaning in what each dream presents. Sometimes the insights bring joy, and sometimes they bring despair, which can lead to greater understanding. These dreams had an immense impact on me when I first encountered them. In the stillness of the night, they surprised, puzzled and disturbed me. In my Hatha Yoga classes and in my work in general, I have greater compassion for my pupils as well as a greater understanding of their spiritual and psychological needs. It is my hope that in offering these dreams, you will benefit from them as I did in sharing them with my teacher.

In our Sufi tradition, dreams and stories are considered a very important part of the training. The teaching stories which came through some of my dreams have an individual as well as a collective message or meaning. A literal understanding of the dreams is not necessary because they work more on feelings than the mind. Every one of these dreams I took to my teacher; some she wanted to share only with me, others with the group. Mrs. Tweedie said, we meet at night because at night the mind is still, the body's still, and in this silence we can experience the truth of God.

The reason why I do not explain all the dreams is because often the meanings can change as we are changing and progressing through life. However I do explain some of these dreams in terms of their significance to me.

∞

Finding the Teacher

The following dream I consider to be the most important I ever had. It happened shortly after meeting Mrs. Tweedie. At the time I found the experience of this dream very confusing. When I told the dream to Mrs. Tweedie, she then immediately knew exactly what it meant and she said, "Miriam, I now know what to do with you," which meant that she would from now on be taking me on as one of her disciples.

~

As I was sleeping, I felt the crown of my head opening; there was a small hole, the size of an average coin. Then Mrs. Tweedie sat on top of my head and entered into my body through this hole three times, up and down. When she came up the first time, she suddenly turned into a mountain, and then she changed back into Mrs. Tweedie and went into my body again and, when she came out, she suddenly turned into an ocean. Then the ocean suddenly changed back into Mrs. Tweedie again. Then suddenly she turned into a bat and entered my body again. When the bat exited through my head, it turned back into Mrs. Tweedie.

~

Mrs. Tweedie interpreted this dream as follows. She said the mountain signifies spiritual height, and you need a guide to climb the mountain. The ocean represents the collective unconscious which I needed to enter, and the fact that I needed a teacher to help me understand. The bat represents the night, because Mrs.

Tweedie's teaching was usually done during the night. The other significant factor here is the number three, because Mrs. Tweedie entered my body three times. It is common in spiritual training that a disciple goes to a master three times before being accepted.

∞

After seven months with Mrs. Tweedie I had the following dream.

~

The Young Doctor

A young doctor had a meditation group and I was involved with this group. He said, "Nobody can come into this group unless he is relaxed. So every student must have a reflexology treatment before he can enter the group." I replied, "It takes nearly an hour to give a treatment." He replied, "Give one for only fifteen minutes so that you can treat four people in an hour." There were eight people in the group. I had to treat all those people before the meditation could start. That same night I saw myself outside of my body very clearly. I realized that this was a very significant dream.

~

Mrs. Tweedie told me that she didn't know how to interpret this dream but that I would know the interpretation in the future. A few years later, I totally understood it. Three or four years after that I met a young doctor with the same name as the man in my dream. He came to me privately for Yoga once or twice a week for about two years. He had a lot of problems and I did some relaxation therapy with him. One day I went to Mrs. Tweedie's and there he was. Mrs. Tweedie gave him a lot of attention. A few weeks later she asked, "Why don't you do a meditation group together?" We used to meet often to discuss how he wanted me to do reflexology in his practice. But he had so many problems that nothing really came of all our plans. Yet a few years later, when I already had a meditation group, he came and was part of it for a while. Looking back, I feel that this experience and the connection with the young doctor were deeply significant in starting me off with the meditation group that used to meet regularly at my house.

I was very restless and extremely possessive of Mrs. Tweedie all the time. I was always cooking for her—but just one portion, never anything for the group—just for her. I realized I was getting too possessive. Perhaps because of this and for many others reasons Mrs. Tweedie was very angry with me. But, the angrier she became, the more I loved her and, unfortunately, the more possessive I became as well. This is unusual for me, because I never reacted to someone else's anger in this way. Generally it's easy to make me angry and it seemed at this time that she either reprimanded me or ignored me, but again, the more she ignored me, the closer to her I felt. Even if she didn't talk to me, I knew deep down that somewhere she was holding me and loving me. I came to realize very quickly that nothing that happened around Mrs. Tweedie was what it appeared to be on the surface. Even when she was erupting in anger, she remained steeped in compassion.

~

One day when I was going through so much trouble and felt so miserable and vulnerable, I couldn't do anything but cry. Mrs. Tweedie said to me, "Some human souls are so tender. They need to be looked after like a newborn baby." Other people were there, but I knew she had meant it for me. I melted.

∞

Visit to the King

Guruji appeared to me in a dream and asked me to come to him. I went and he was such a tremendous power, like a fountain of energy exploding in the top of my head. It was like I had water splashing all over my head. I was floating out of my body with him in space and he pulled me more and more. He said, "Let's go to the Beloved." It was really indescribable—like drifting in space, yet pulled by some kind of very powerful force. All of a sudden the face of a shaven, strong-faced Oriental man appeared. I started walking with him and together we went on a donkey. Later we were each on our own donkeys. We journeyed for days, never exchanging even a word. We were always welcomed at the different villages we passed through. A mountain appeared in the distance, and he said, "Let's go up the mountain." We walked for quite some time, then he told me to get off the donkey and keep walking by myself. He said, "Go to the king. He's waiting for you." And I was left alone. When I reached the king, he was absolutely glorious in silver and gold and sitting on a throne. Absolute splendour! The king said, "I have waited for you for such a long time." I explained, "We were walking for a long time and all the people along the way delayed us." There was another golden throne next to him and he sat me on it. He said, "It's good to have you here." And I replied, "It is glorious to be here." I looked out at all the clouds then looked down and I saw Mrs. Tweedie's tiny room with people sitting there. I was one of them. I was so amazed to see this and suddenly he said, "Go back the same way you came up."

~

I told Mrs. Tweedie about this dream and she said, "You're blessed."

∞

Following a few depressing days I went to Mrs. Tweedie and made the resolution not to see her so often and to become less attached to her. I meditated at her house and saw pages of papers in a foreign language flashing before me. I couldn't read them. I told her about this and she said I would be getting a message in the course of time as to what this dream means. I felt terribly empty, yet very alert at the same time and not so tired. I was less attached to everyone near me and I had less pain in my heart and a lot more vigour. The following day I had this dream.

~

The Journey Home

I dreamed that I planned to go on a trip with some people. We had to meet in a particular place and I arrived there early. I told the group I had to go home to collect something, but instead, I started to tidy up the house and, when I looked at my watch, it was 8:10 and the bus was supposed to leave at 8:00. I hurried to catch up and when I got there, I could see the bus in the distance. They had left me behind. I met two old ladies near a bridge and I told them that I had missed the bus, and they said to me that, if I went down these stairs, that I might meet up with the group on the other side of the tunnel. The place looked terribly familiar to me. I woke up before I caught up with the group and realized that I had never left home at all.

~

Mrs. Tweedie was very pleased with this dream and said, "You take yourself with you wherever you go." In other words, my home is with me ... everywhere I go. Another difficult period followed and I felt like accusing her of not caring for me any more. I felt terribly sorry for myself and that she cared for everyone else but me. Then I had the following dream.

~

A Big Lion

A big lion came to me. It was quite affectionate. And, as it happens, I have always loved lions. I put a leather collar around his neck and a leash and went for a walk with him. I began to speak to the lion as if it was Mrs. Tweedie and I suddenly realized that it really *was* her. We were walking and the lion was trying to free himself from me, but he couldn't. Even though I didn't hold the leash tightly, it just couldn't run away. We had a great time in rivers, meadows and fields and then the lion pulled away, but instead of leaving, he stopped and waited for me to get hold of the leash again. It was a wonderful outing and a lovely experience.

~

My interpretation of this dream is that if one holds a bird in one's hand and lets it go free, if it comes back to you, it's yours; but if it never comes back, it was never yours.

∞

I felt very calm over the next few days. My family and I were on holiday in St. Ives. The place is pretty and I love the sea. It always makes me happy. I had a new feeling of inner peace that was hard to explain. I seemed to have contacted an empty place inside. My meditation was becoming deeper and I could tell when I was about to go into it or come out of it. Sometimes I had a choking sensation in my throat. I loved the experience of knowing what's going on in *dhyana* ("the abstraction of the senses," said to be a joining of the individual mind with the Universal Mind). It felt as if something in me was expanding. I felt as though *I am* nothing, floating in infinite space. My body felt so very light and there seemed to be no end to my awareness. When I came out of it, I felt different. I was still getting irritated with my Lennie, but it felt so superficial. I was never affected "inside."

I was a vegetarian but I didn't want to make any changes at home. I felt I had to be completely private about what was happening to me. I didn't talk to anyone in my family about these things and not even to Lennie.

The longing was taking on a different form. I gazed into the ocean and I felt at peace. Over the next few days I felt no physical or emotional pain. I thanked God for this feeling of freedom and contentment. Yet I still had many doubts about Mrs. Tweedie's meditation group. I only had a good feeling from one person. I thought she was very spiritual. Most of the conversations in the group were so mundane. But what bothered me even more was that I was not getting any spiritual instruction. There had to be a reason for this.

I never thought spiritual life would be like this—so full of longing, pain, frustration and love. I never imagined I could feel such love. I knew it was not just for Mrs. Tweedie. It was for something beyond her—something I still didn't understand.

The Retreat

I dreamed that I was called to go on a retreat for three months. Five rabbis and their wives started a breakaway movement and they were excommunicated from the Jewish religion because of their new ideas. They asked me to go on a retreat and my husband said it was all right for me to go. I hadn't told Mrs. Tweedie about it. Twenty people joined the movement. We were told to prepare for a very hard routine of religious study, penance, fasting, physical work and meditation. We accepted the challenge with love. I was afraid to tell Mrs. Tweedie about it so I sent a message with someone from the group. She asked me to come and see her immediately. I went to her and she told me she was coming with me. She said, "I shall close the centre for three months so I can share this experience with you."

~

When I told Mrs. Tweedie this dream, she said the number ten (five rabbis and their wives) represented change and rebirth. Twenty (people in the movement) was a combination of two and zero. Two is a symbol of creation, and zero refers to the Absolute. It also stands for resurrection and judgment. Three (three months) refers to the feminine and to the instincts.

∞

It was the Jewish New Year and, unlike previous years, I was looking forward to going to the Synagogue. I was filled with joy as if the creation of the world was happening inside me. At one point in the service I started to feel very high. I felt as though Guruji, Mrs. Tweedie and I were merging into one being. Soon the whole congregation became part of our oneness and I never felt such happiness. Tremendous heat came over me, and I collapsed into a chair. It's impossible to explain what was happening inside me: peace, light, oneness all at once. Suddenly I realized it had nothing to do with the ritual of the holiday or the Synagogue. It was from somewhere else. I hoped I could keep this feeling alive in me forever! Thank you, Mrs. Tweedie, I thought. I never knew so much love existed. Thank you, thank you, thank you.

∞

Mrs. Tweedie Away

Mrs. Tweedie left abruptly without telling anyone how long she would be away. She had hinted a few times that she might do something like this.

I dreamed she was in a warm country, maybe India, with a young-looking Indian man, who was wearing glasses. They were walking in a garden. I saw white roses and a white house in the distance. They seemed to be discussing something very important. I felt that Mrs. Tweedie was very well and hoped that she would come back soon.

~

Mrs. Tweedie was gone for three months. She returned to her flat on the 13th January, 1981. She had been in India just as my dream indicated. She stayed by herself for two weeks and wouldn't see anyone. She wanted to be in silence.

∞

The Parcel

I dreamed that I was in a room with a woman, who handed me a parcel which she said Mrs. Tweedie wanted me to have. I opened it to find a pair of old boots. "What am I going to do with these?" I asked her. "Throw them away," she said. I looked again. There was something else in the box—old photographs from my childhood. All of a sudden, Mrs. Tweedie came into the room and she looked very old.

"When can I come to see you?" I asked.

"Any time you like," was her response.

I started to cry. She kissed my forehead and comforted me.

~

Boots or shoes often represent ideas concerning destiny. The old photographs here are representative of the past.

∞

Oil

Guruji came to my house. "Let's go," he said.
"Where are we going?" I asked
"To a prayer house," he replied.
We walked very quickly and came to my Synagogue. Guruji sat next to the rabbi and I sat in the ladies' gallery. Guruji called to me from across the Synagogue: "Pray a lot," he said. When the service was over, Guruji said, "You're going to get a lot of oil!" I turned around and all of a sudden, he wasn't Guruji anymore, he was Mrs. Tweedie.

~

When I told Mrs. Tweedie about this dream, she knew what it meant. She told me that I have been blessed. Oil is a symbol for initiation.

∞

Ten years before I met Mrs. Tweedie I had the first dream in what was to become my extraordinary dream-life:

~

A Preparation

I was called to go on a training course in the Himalayan mountains. I had to leave my husband and family behind. All I was allowed to bring with me were a few clothes and some paper and pencils. I was to be gone for two years and I was not going to be able to contact my family. I arrived at the site where my training was to take place. It was a plateau with goats, chickens and deer wandering about. A group of women were busily at work. They looked as though they belonged to the same family. I saw a little house and I was told to go in as if I was expected. A small man was inside, sitting on the floor. He told me to sit next to him. He couldn't speak English but we were able to understand one another perfectly, exchanging my English for his strange language. We talked for a long time, had some food, and then he gave me a series of instructions. When he finished, he showed me the tent where he said I'd be living. I understood that he would be my teacher and that I would be following a very tough regime of early morning risings, cold ritual baths, followed by hours of Hatha Yoga, meditation, hard manual work and very little food. I would have to write down all my experiences. All of a sudden I felt hungry and alone. In spite of that I decided to stay.

I saw the old man quite a bit. Sometimes we'd go for sunrise walks up to the mountain. He taught me about solitude and silence and how to be on my own. I learned to master my physical body. Two years passed. He told me it was time to go home and that I would never see him again.

~

I told Mrs. Tweedie this dream when I first met her and she asked me if I ever had any other dreams.

~

One day, while I was meditating at Mrs. Tweedie's flat, I saw masses of deformed souls coming toward me. It was a frightening experience and, when I told her about it, she said she often saw them too. She told me that souls from lower planes are always attracted to spiritual groups. "But we are protected," she said, "so don't worry about it."

∞

Guruji

I dreamed I was only twenty-six years old (I was forty-six at the time). Guruji appeared to me and asked me to come to him every day. He was very friendly and affectionate. He said he would tell me a story every day. So I went to his garden and we sat there under a mango tree. He was dressed all in white and sat on a bench. I sat on the ground next to his feet.

~

The following is the first of many stories Guruji told me.

~

Babu

Once there was a very rich man. He had ten children whom he loved and cherished. He gave them the best education possible and saw to all their needs and comforts. But for some reason they never loved or respected him. One day he took a walk down a country road and found a little boy wandering all alone. He was an orphan, and when he looked into the man's eyes and said, "Babu (Daddy)," the man's heart melted. He felt so sorry for the boy that he took him home and adopted him. This infuriated the family, who thought he loved this boy more than his own children. The boy felt unwelcome in the house and followed the man everywhere.

One day, Babu said to the little boy, "I don't know why they are so jealous of you. You are such a nice, quiet and obedient child." He called the family together and told them, "Look here, I am a rich man and I am going to divide my wealth among all of you." Even though he had given them everything, they still didn't like having the boy around. There was only one thing left to do. He gathered the family together again and said, "I've given you everything I've got, but still there is no peace or harmony at home so I am going away."

He collected a few things together and he and the boy set out on a long journey. The great love between them was apparent to everyone who met them. Time passed. They wandered from place to place and began to run out of money. The boy adored the old man and promised to look after him until the end. The years of wandering took their toll and the father became weak and fell ill. He felt he was about to die. When he told the boy this he wept. "Babu, Babu," he pleaded. "Stay with me." "I have to go," Babu whispered. "But when I die, you will only have to remember me and I will be with you."

~

There are various symbolic meanings in this dream: In ancient Indian tradition, when a householder finishes his family duties and his work, he finds a spiritual teacher who he stays with until he dies. The orphan child signifies purity, innocence and surrender, and his own children represent the material world which he has to let go of to find truth. You cannot be a prophet in your own home.

∞

Guruji kept his promise to tell me a story every day. Every night in my dreams he would tell me at least one and sometimes three stories. I was exhausted. When I told Mrs. Tweedie about the dreams, she said there were many more to come. Every time I came to her house, she asked me, "Any dreams?" And I usually had one to tell her.

∞

The Invisible Elephant

A beggar was wandering on a road lost in his thoughts. He sensed that someone was following him, but when he looked around, no one was there. This puzzled him. "When I look ahead of me, I can distinctly hear someone walking behind me," he thought, "but when I turn around, no one is there."

This went on for a long time. One evening he decided to challenge his unseen companion. "Whoever you are, please stop playing tricks on me. Tell me who you are." He turned around, but again no one was there. Then he heard a voice. "It is an elephant," it said. And indeed, he could feel the presence of an elephant even though he couldn't see one. This time, the invisible elephant spoke and he told the beggar to climb on his back. "I'm going to take you on a very long journey," he said. And off they went. The beggar was confused by this strange turn of events. But he and his invisible companion became fast friends and shared their deepest thoughts and feelings.

The elephant walked and walked toward a distant ashram. When he got to the gate, he asked the beggar to get off his back and sit down. The beggar did as he was told and the elephant left him there. The beggar waited by the ashram gate and the swamis took him inside. They fed and looked after him. One day a teacher approached him. Other beggars were sitting there too, but the teacher singled him out and told him to follow him inside. The teacher asked him a lot of questions. One question was, "Do you want to beg or to serve?"

"I want to serve," answered the beggar without hesitation. The swami told him of many other wonderful things he could do, but the beggar stuck to his conviction: "I only want to serve."

~

The elephant represents a drive or energy in a transition process from begging to service. We came to this life with two attributes, to serve and to worship.

∞

The Little Princess

A beautiful young princess lived in a palace. The king and queen had been told they would be childless, but they prayed with great feeling and their prayers were answered. Their little daughter was so lovely they just couldn't do enough for her. They fulfilled her every desire. But no matter what she was given, the little princess was always sad. The king and queen offered her endless gifts to cheer her up: birds, miniature zoos, animals, games, but nothing seemed to make her happy.

One day the princess ran through an opening in the palace gate and she was amazed by what she saw: Children!—other children playing, dancing and singing. She loved everything about their world and she wanted to be part of it. She got back to the palace before anyone noticed she had gone.

The princess devised a plan. "The next time I go out," she thought, "I'll disguise myself so nobody will know who I am." It worked. She was able to slip out and play with the other children without anyone noticing. This went on for weeks. Then one day, the king and queen found what she was up to and punished her severely. The princess didn't care. It was worth it. From that very first moment she had felt total freedom outside the palace gate and she was never unhappy again.

~

One is conditioned or imprisoned in life, but once one has experienced freedom, nothing can take it away from you.

~

Immediately after this dream I had an experience in which Guruji took me to the Ganges River and dipped me into the water three times and then we did our *japa* together. (A *japa* is a spiritual discipline involving the meditative repetition of a mantra or the name of a divine power.)

∞

The Three Boons

A beggar had been wandering in the wilderness for a long time. One day he realized how tired he was and stopped under a tree to rest. It was a very hot day, but the shade of the tree protected him. There he sat, lost in his thoughts. Suddenly, he heard a voice coming from the tree. It said, "I shall give you three boons." The beggar looked all around him. There was no one in sight. The voice repeated the offer three times. The beggar was scared, but he answered anyway. "Tell me what the boons are and I will choose," he said. The voice agreed and the choices were offered. "You can have a big diamond, a large stone, or the River of Life." The beggar tried to make up his mind. "If I take the diamond and try to sell it," he thought, "people will see I am a beggar and think I stole it. Nobody will give me anything for it. I could even end up in jail. As for the stone, it is just too heavy. What could I do with it? But the River of Life will quench my thirst and clean me." So that's what he chose, and the voice said, "It is yours." The beggar sat under the tree for three years. He never needed anything because the River of Life sustained him. One day, the voice returned. "Why do you stay here?" it asked. "You can take the River of Life anywhere you go. You have meditated here for three years now. But, wherever you go, the River of Life will be with you." The beggar didn't want to leave, as he was very comfortable under the tree. Eventually though he got up and followed the suggestion of the voice to take the River of Life out into the world.

~

I understood this dream to mean that the life force will take you wherever you have to go.

∞

Another dream followed.

~

Climbing the Mountain

A group of people decided to climb a mountain. Some set out on foot, some on horseback and others in horse-drawn carts. They all wanted to reach the peak, but before they got very far a carriage with four horses came right out of nowhere and sped past them all. It shot up the mountain and went right out of sight. The mountain climbers wondered who the people in the carriage were and how it could move so fast. They were amazed by what they had seen as they continued on their way.

~

I think this dream interprets as Mrs. Tweedie quickening up my journey to enlightenment.

∞

I had the following dream about Guruji:

~

Setting Sun

He and I were sitting under a mango tree. "Let's go to the River Ganges," he said. And so we went. We stood on the riverbank looking at the people in the water; then he asked me, "Do you think there are any saints in the water?" "I really don't know how to distinguish a saint standing in the water," I answered. "Look! Look! Look!" he urged me. But I didn't know what to look for and so I couldn't tell if there were any saints there or not. Guruji suggested that we go into the water ourselves. We went quite far beyond all the people so that if we turned around we could only see their backs. Guruji dipped me into the water three times and said, "Now find a saint." But all I could see now was a distant collection of backs, necks and heads. If there was a saint in there somewhere, it was beyond me. Guruji was standing to the left of me and I suddenly felt a strong vibration coming from the right. I told him and we both looked as far as our eyes could see, but nobody was there. All we saw was the setting sun.

Guruji and I walked out of the water and went back to his house. We resumed our places under the mango tree. "Do you want a story?" he asked. "Yes, of course I do," I replied. This is what he told me: "A man came to me and said, 'Teacher, how does one become a scholar?' This question was surprising, but he thought for a moment and gave the first answer that came into his mind. 'Go and explore the Thousand Isles,' he advised. 'After that, you will surely have learned a lot and you will be a scholar.'

"The question wasn't asked out of curiosity. This man really did want to become a scholar. So he did as the teacher suggested, and went to explore the Thousand Isles. After several years of traveling and studying, he came back. The teacher questioned him for a long time and sensed his dissatisfaction. 'Yes, it's true,' the man said. 'I don't think I'm a scholar yet.'

"The teacher thought for a while and suggested that he climb Mount Everest. 'Observe everything carefully,' he advised. 'Notice especially the differences in the people and the vegetation due to the high altitude.' The man followed the teacher's advice to the letter and returned to share what he had learned. Several years had passed and the teacher was very happy to see him again. He questioned him for a long time, and while he was pleased with the answers he heard, the man still didn't think he had become the scholar he so longed to be.

"This time, the teacher sent him to a special library, which housed an extraordinary collection of books. He told him to touch the cover of every book, and all the knowledge they contained would be transmitted to him. As before, the man did exactly as he was told. But there were so many books it took years just to touch them all. When he lifted his fingers from the very last book, he headed straight for the teacher. Their meeting was no different from previous ones. 'I must admit I have taken in an enormous amount of knowledge,' he said. 'But I still cannot honestly claim to be a scholar.'

"The teacher told his student to stay with him for twelve years, promising to teach him what he wanted to know. And so for twelve years the man lived with his teacher and served him. But the teacher didn't teach him a single thing. When twelve years had passed, the teacher sent him out into the world. 'If people gather around you,' he said, 'and you know what to say to them on each occasion, then you will know that you indeed are a teacher.'

"The man set out on his own and sure enough, wherever he went, he attracted a crowd of people. 'I wanted to be a scholar,' he thought, 'but I think I have turned into a teacher.'"

~

This is a very complex dream. It is a dream within a dream. On a simple level the first part is about awareness. The second part deals with knowledge that the mind can not know.

∞

Another dream followed on quickly:

~

A Company of Saints

A company of great saints sat around a huge round table: Rabbi Hillel, Rabbi Shamai, Rabbi Akkiba, Rabbi Ben Zachai, Rabbi Nachman and Guruji. They were discussing an important page in the *Torah*. I approached them, very pleased to see Guruji in the company of what, were to me, the greatest saints of all time. Guruji looked at me and said, "I called you and you didn't want to come to me. I need you. I called you a second time and you came. You need me."

A very serious discussion transpired in which it was decided that everyone at the table would disguise himself as a human being in order to help humanity. Each one of us would be sent to a different part of the world. Guruji would dress as a beggar and go to Jerusalem. I was assigned to go with him. Guruji was dressed in white and I was in black. We both carried handkerchiefs in our hands, which indicated that we were not begging for ourselves. "We will get to know the world according to how people live," he told me. We sat and begged for days and we did very well. "If you beg or ask for others," Guruji said, "it is given." A discussion developed between us and I said, "Charity begins at home."

"Yes," said Guruji, "but duty also starts at home. Honour you father and mother. If this edict was obeyed, there wouldn't be any trouble in the world." On another occasion, when we were begging together, he said to me, "Love is to give and pain is to take."

We begged and sat together for many years. And again a gathering of the saints was arranged. They had to report on what they had found out about the nature of human suffering. Rabbi Akkiba began the proceedings. Addressing the other saints, he said, "Dear Friends, you keep the scales of humanity in balance. God is guiding you to help all humanity. By giving we receive."

∞

The Saint and the Servant

A saint had five daughters and one son. The boy was born crippled, but oh, how the saint loved him. He taught him everything he knew. They were not only father and son, they were very close friends. One day, the boy asked, "Father, why did God create me like this?"

"God created you in his own image," the saint answered. "This is the way he wants you to be. He doesn't love you any less because of your handicap. God creates all men in his own image and each of us is unique."

The boy had very little to say to this. He was quite frail and, after only twenty years of life, he died. The entire household mourned the loss. Everyone, that is, but the saint. When his disciples came to console him, they found him laughing and talking and telling tales. And, when the saint ordered a great feast, they thought that in his grief he must have gone mad. They didn't know what to do.

The saint saw what was going on and called them all around him. "You think I'm mad," he said, "but you are all wrong. I will tell you a story and, if you understand it, you will know why I am rejoicing."

This is the story he told them: "Once there was a poor and lonely man. He searched and searched for work and eventually he got a job as a servant in a rich household. His master was severe and demanding. He had to work day and night and, when he slept, it was in a simple hut. Many years of hard work passed.

"One day, the master called the servant to his house. 'I've watched you over the years,' he said. 'I know you are a hardworking, faithful and obedient servant. Listen to me carefully. I have to go away on a long business journey. I may be gone for many, many years, and I want you to take over my household. Move into my house, become the master of the house, and do as you like.'

"The servant couldn't believe his good fortune. He promised his master he would continue to serve him and to do all the work that he did before. The rich man left and the servant moved in, living in great comfort. But he never forgot who he was. He kept working. He made improvements in the house and in the garden, always taking his responsibilities very seriously. It became well known throughout the land how beautiful the house had become under his care. Yet the servant remained humble.

"After twenty years the master set out on his journey home. On the way he heard that his house had been turned into a beautiful palace. When he arrived home, he praised the servant for all the wonderful work he had performed but that now he would have to move out of the house and back into the hut.

"The servant replied, 'I don't mind at all. I have had twenty years of joy and happiness.'"

∞

Initiation Story

In my next dream I was sitting with Guruji under the mango tree when he suggested in Hindi that we go to the mountain. So off we went and, before we got very far, a terrible storm hit. Our clothes were light and flimsy. We ran through the rain and howling wind and finally we found shelter in a cave.

"You can't go to sleep yet," he said. "I shall bless you first and give you your *mantra*." He said the *mantra* aloud and I repeated it three times. Then I lost consciousness. Indescribable things happened then. I was struck by a kind of light, heat and pain—all mixed together. I don't know how long this lasted, but when I regained consciousness, I didn't feel like *me*. We were still in the cave and Guruji was staring hard at me. "The storm is over," he said. "Let's go on." We left the cave and continued on up the mountain. At one point he turned to me and asked, "What would happen to you if I pushed you down?"

"Well, I'd fall down and die," I replied.

"Do you mind if I do push you down?" he asked.

I told him that I wouldn't mind at all. So he pushed me and I rolled down to the bottom of the mountain. I was unhurt. I walked back to the top of the mountain and he said, "You see things don't always turn out as you expect them to. Stay here alone. I have to return home."

I begged him not to leave me alone on the mountain. I was so afraid of being lonely and sad. But my pleas did not dissuade him. Guruji left me and I stayed behind. I was alone for a very long time. Eventually, I returned to his house to find him there waiting for me. "Do you want to hear another story now?" he asked. I replied that I did.

"A man had to attend to some business in a distant town. He took a few things with him and set out on his donkey. Right from the beginning the donkey gave him trouble. Sometimes it refused to walk any faster than at a snail's pace. At other times it would just stop and wouldn't walk at all. It didn't take long before the man was fed up. He cursed the animal and proceeded towards his destination on foot. After some time the donkey caught up with him. The man climbed on its back and on they went. They reached a village square where a terrible quarrel was taking place. The head of the village approached and asked the man to help settle it. But he didn't want to get involved. 'I'm not a judge,' he said. 'I'm only passing by. Please leave me out of your quarrels.' All of a sudden the donkey let out such a loud roar that all the people in the square stopped quarrelling and ran, frightened, back to their homes. The man was puzzled by the donkey's behaviour, but didn't spend too much time wondering about it. It was getting late and they had to find a place to sleep. They found an inn and, after a good night's sleep, some people from the village brought food for him and the donkey. They wanted to express their gratitude for what had happened the day before. The villagers invited them to stay on in the village. But the man declined, as he had business in another town.

"The man and his donkey continued their journey. When they reached a waterfall, the man realized that he was very tired. He stopped to rest for a while. When he had eaten, he lay down and fell into a deep sleep. While he was sleeping, two robbers approached them. But the donkey roared so loudly that they gave up their evil intentions and ran away. When the man woke up, he was unaware of what had happened. All he knew was that he couldn't find the donkey. This made him angry as he would now have to go the rest of the way on foot. He walked for many days and became tired, hungry and dirty. Then, all of a sudden and out of nowhere, the donkey appeared at the side of the road. The donkey was so happy to see his master that he nuzzled up against him. The man was also *very* pleased to see the donkey. He climbed onto its back. This time the donkey stayed with him quite obediently until they reached a town."

~

There are three stories here. It's like a Russian doll where there's a dream within a dream within a dream. The first dream, where I go to the mountains with Guruji. The mountains signify spiritual heights. The storm represents disruption, in terms of anticipation of something unknown. He was talking in Hindi to challenge my Western mode of thought, which is to question everything. The sudden tiredness that came over me represents the fact that I was still too much in my mind and not letting go. Pushing me down the mountain was a test of surrender and faith. The fact that things do not happen as one expects is an important fact of life. Things are as they are and everything happens for a reason. Guruji leaves me alone in order for me to digest what had happened to me. The donkey in Guruji's next story represents stubbornness. The donkey stops and starts and goes its own stubborn way, and this represents ego, or not letting go and always wanting to be in control. But on a spiritual path, one has to be free. The fact that the man walks on regardless of the donkey's behaviour signifies determination to just carry on to reach the goal, or destination. The fight in the village square signifies my fears, and the donkey's roar signifies a wake-up call. The robbers represent the need to let go of attachments. The fact that the robbers didn't take anything shows that the man's essence, or true value, cannot be taken.

∞

My next dream involved Mrs. Tweedie again.

~

A Trip to India

We went on a trip to India. As soon as we arrived a series of unexpected events took place. First we lost our luggage, then our passports disappeared, and finally our money was gone, leaving us penniless. There we were, in a strange country with no identification what-soever: We started to wander around, looking for food and a place to rest. We came to a river and sat down. A flock of blackbirds came over to welcome us. They wanted us to feel as free as they were free. We decided to stay at that spot and the birds kept us company most of the time. I found a little bowl and began to beg for rice. Whatever I received I gave to Mrs. Tweedie. I became thinner and thinner until there wasn't much more to my body than its skeleton. Yet Mrs. Tweedie still looked very well.

We had planned to stay in India for two months, but by that time two years had passed and we decided we must go back to England. So, we said goodbye to the river, our dwelling and to our friends, the blackbirds, and began our journey to the airport. On the way, we bumped into a friend who helped us get to England. When we arrived there, Mrs. Tweedie's flat was occu-pied so she moved into my house. She stayed with me until her flat was ready for her to move back in.

~

After this, things changed between us. When Mrs. Tweedie heard this dream, she said to me, "It takes two years to understand what's going on here." My first two years with Mrs. Tweedie were the hardest. This dream signified to her that I was ready to be pushed even harder. She became more critical about everything I did and said.

∞

My next dream involved Guruji.

~

Magic Carpet

He and I were sitting in his garden when suddenly a huge crowd of people swarmed around us. I thought that we'd suffocate. But then everyone bowed down to us and, while their heads were down, a magic carpet appeared and lifted us up. Nobody even saw it happen. We landed in a village where three women, who looked very poor, waited for us. One had a baby on her back. The second carried a bag of food on her shoulders, and the third had a jug of water on her head. The one with the baby told us to follow her and we did as she asked. After we had walked for a long time, we saw a beautiful white building in the distance. Standing outside were what appeared to be shadows of people, although they might have been ghosts. We decided to go inside but, when we got there, we found it wasn't a building at all, but an empty shell. There was simply nothing there. We sat on the ground and the "shadow people" followed us.

They expected Guruji to give a talk. But he sang a song instead. All the "shadows" started to hum at the same time. Then Guruji turned to me and said, "Let's go." While they carried on humming, we left on the magic carpet and again nobody noticed our departure.

~

This Magic Carpet dream is a mystery dream about something that has to be done or redeemed.

∞

My next dream was something I experienced in my meditation.

~

A Riddle

Guruji came into my room and sat on my bed. He said, "Miriam, I am going to give you a riddle to work out: Three birds are flying in the sky; one is white and one is black, but what colour is the third one?" I thought about it and then I answered, "Well, it could be white or black, or maybe it's both colours, or even grey." "Try harder," he said. So I did. But every time I gave an answer, he just told me to "Try harder." After three or four guesses, I gave up. "How do you know there were three birds?" Guruji asked. "Have you seen them?" "No," I admitted. "I haven't seen them, but as *you* said there were three birds, I accepted it." Guruji continued to tease me. "Birds are only *Maya* (illusion), and *Maya* can disguise itself in any number." He continued to encourage me to figure out the riddle, but I still didn't get it. He just laughed and laughed until finally, he said, "It's your riddle. Work it out." Then, he got up, touched my forehead, and left.

~

When I told Mrs. Tweedie about this experience, she immediately knew the answer to the riddle. "The third bird was gold," she told me. "It was reflecting the light of the sun." She told me to tell this interpretation to Guruji the next time he came to me. I did and, by the smile on his face, I knew it was the right answer.

∞

Photos and Chains

I dreamed that I was in a beautiful country home. I was sitting in a room with a very high ceiling. It was completely empty apart from a big four-poster bed, yet somehow it was still quite grand. Hundreds of photographs of Mrs. Tweedie were plastered on the wall. Each one was the same. There was a big fireplace opposite the bed with a chair inside it. That's where I was sitting and I was in chains. I couldn't go anywhere. I couldn't visit Mrs. Tweedie, yet I was quite peaceful and happy. My jailers told me if I got rid of the photos, I would be allowed to sleep in a comfortable bed and go to see Mrs. Tweedie any time I wanted. But I wasn't willing to give them up.

One day someone from Mrs. Tweedie's meditation group came to visit me to see how I was. I didn't want to speak to her. She told me she thought I looked very well under the circumstances. I told her I hadn't slept for days. "I just close my eyes and think of Mrs. Tweedie," I said, "and immediately I fall into meditation. It makes me feel so refreshed that I don't really have to sleep." Right after she left, Mrs. Tweedie came in. She had passed the jailers without being noticed. She released me from my chains. "You can stay with me forever in my house," she whispered.

~

Photos and chains is about attachment followed by integration.

∞

In my next dream Guruji appeared to me again.

~

Instructions for the Group

Guruji was looking very stern. He announced, "Maidens and men of the group, in six months all of you should marry and take on your responsibilities as real Sufis. Build your homes, raise your families and do your craft and your work as you always did. We Sufis live in the world and we do our duties just as our ancestors did. We keep our feet firmly on the ground and the vault of the sky will protect us. Our heads are supported by the Divine Power. I shall call you in your need and protect you wherever you are. God be with you."

~

When I told Mrs. Tweedie this dream, she said it wasn't for me. She instructed me to tell it to the group on Friday evening. Later she typed up Guruji's exact instructions and sent copies to everyone she thought should have these important teachings.

∞

Manuscript

I found myself in a primitive and ancient house. An old man was sitting on the floor. I couldn't see his face, but he seemed to be Mongolian and he wore a Persian headdress. He told me that during some trouble in his country he had lost a manuscript he had written. It was important to re-write it and he asked me to do this for him. I told him it would be quite easy for me and I re-wrote the manuscript without any difficulty even though it was in Persian, which is a language I don't understand. Suddenly I was in Mrs. Tweedie's kitchen, sitting at a table. "For the next five hours," she announced, "there must be absolute silence." She did this so that I could write. I wrote out the manuscript in Persian and, when it was finished, it was a large book. Mrs. Tweedie took it in her hands with great reverence. After holding it for some time she said, "It must be translated into English." And it was done.

Safad

Mrs. Tweedie, a friend and I went on a trip to the ancient mystical city of Safad in Israel. We made our way through narrow streets until a man approached us. He must have been about sixty or seventy years old. He was dressed in an ordinary grey suit, but he had a tremendous dignity about him. He was full of light. He asked Mrs. Tweedie and me to come to his house. My friend was not invited, so we left her standing by the gate and went down a series of alleys and stairways to his house. The room we entered was scarcely finished with just a bench next to the wall, and the odd chair. The oil lamp hanging in a recess in the wall and the candle on the table provided the only illumination apart from the light emanating from this man. He looked at us and asked, "Are you ready?" I was so scared. I took hold of Mrs. Tweedie's hand and held it tight. Suddenly Guruji appeared and he was also full of light. First he spoke to Mrs. Tweedie, and then to us both, saying, "You are safe in this man's company. He can take you to any of the Seven Heavens if he wants to. He is my companion." We stayed with him and he showed us and taught us many things, all in Guruji's presence. All the while I was holding Mrs. Tweedie's hand. After two weeks, we were told to go. But before we left, we promised not to talk to anybody about what had happened.

Our friend didn't know what had become of us and thought we might be dead. When we finally emerged, we saw a note she had written perhaps days before, telling us she had to leave but would be back. When we got to the gate, she was there waiting for us. She wanted to take us on a trip, but we just wanted to go home.

~

In this dream, the strange man is Guruji himself. He can only take me to the Seven Heavens if I am ready and have surrendered. Safad is an ancient Jewish mystical town. The greatest mystical Jewish teachers came from there.

∞

From Two Eggs

I dreamed that I lived in a cottage at the foot of a tall mountain. Guruji came to me and said, "Climb the mountain, but don't fall down." I began to climb. It was very dangerous, but Guruji was with me. He told me I had chosen a difficult way, but I was on the right path. An eagle was flying above my head, showing me the way. It was a tremendous struggle, but finally I reached the top and I went straight to the eagle's nest where I found two very large eggs. I held them in my hands, and Guruji said, "Take them with you and go back to your cottage." And so I did. The way down was smooth and easy. I carried one egg in each hand. Guruji stayed with me and told me to keep the eggs in a warm place for thirty days. I did this and, when the time had passed, they hatched. A beautiful book with gilded pages came out of the first egg and from the second came a pink rose.

~

The egg is a symbol for life. This dream is about continued propagation of love and spiritual knowledge.

∞

My dream life continued with more very powerful dreams. The following is an early dream that reflects my searching for a direction or spiritual path.

~

The Infinite

I was living in my own home where people often gathered while I was asleep. One night I was awakened by noises from downstairs and, still half asleep, I went to see what was going on. I recognized the people I saw down there, but when they saw me I knew right away I wasn't welcome. So I left, and started to wander in the streets. I must have been a strange ghostly sight, walking the dark, snowy streets wearing just a nightgown. Yet somehow, I was unaffected by the cold and darkness. I came upon a group of beggars dressed in rags. They stood in rows on either side of me and extended their empty palms toward me. I didn't know what they wanted, and I felt I had nothing to give, so I kept walking. After some time, I saw two men dressed in black coats and hats, standing and talking on a street corner. It was so dark I couldn't see their faces. By this time I realized I was desperately lost, so I asked if they could tell me how to get home. Without any hesitation, they pointed far into the distance. I looked in that direction, and to my amazement, there was nothing there, just infinite space.

∞

Throughout the period of my intense dream life I always felt supported by Mrs. Tweedie. Often her interpretations were initially difficult to comprehend, but they always helped, and after pondering on them, I was able to understand their meanings and implications.

She had a deep understanding of the spiritual path and the teachings of the masters. She was always an invaluable source of wisdom.

CHAPTER TEN

Coming to Terms

Forgiving and Forgetting

The Germans killed my beloved father Solomon Mannheimer, my brother Marci, and sister Noemi, and many
other relatives and friends. I had a very real animosity
towards this nation and its people, and I had vowed to
myself never to step foot on German territory again.
What they did to my family was unforgivable. I cannot
forgive the criminals who committed these crimes. I
was not even able to forgive the second or third generation of Germans. All Germans were sick as far as I was
concerned.

When I went to Mrs. Tweedie for spiritual training, I never considered that I would have to confront
the most painful issue in my life. There were all kinds
of people in her group seeking the same thing as me.
She was not interested in peoples' backgrounds. If
they had psychological problems, she advised them to
seek a therapist. She chose the people she wanted to
help. I never told her my life history but, because she
was deeply intuitive and highly evolved, she probably
knew it. She certainly knew when she could help. Her
mission in life was to help us to work on ourselves, find

140

ourselves and get nearer to the truth. Her goal was that we should undertake self-realization.

To my horror, Mrs. Tweedie started to make regular trips to Germany. I noticed that she had started to revise her German language skills. Even though she was educated in Vienna, I assumed she probably had a good grasp of the language, but she must have forgotten due to making England her home for so long. I knew she was fluent in French, Italian, and obviously Russian, but she clearly felt she needed to brush up on her German.

It wasn't long after her book, *Daughter of Fire,* was translated into German that an influx of many young Germans started to visit her in London for guidance. I was shocked to see so many Germans at her meetings and became rather jealous that she was spending so much time with them. Some came for a short time and others for longer periods. She had to find accommodation for some of them. I tried to block out these newcomers, but I knew that I had some responsibility to help if I could with accommodation, but my rather trenchant view was that I went to Mrs. Tweedie to learn more about meditation and to be with her, not to be an estate agent! But we had a spare room in our house which we rented out from time to time. So when Mrs. Tweedie asked if Lennie and I would take in a young German visitor, I couldn't say "no." But it came as a bit of a shock. Lennie was very relaxed with the idea, but I struggled with the situation. I could see that there wasn't much point in following Mrs. Tweedie if I wasn't willing to look inside myself to find out why I was resisting her request. So, a young German lady came to stay with us, she was a medieval historian and very cultured. She spoke very good English and I also spoke a little German. I quickly realised that she was a very intelligent and likeable person and we got off to a good start; we became very friendly. I used to drive her to our meetings with Mrs. Tweedie on most days.

This was a period of great change for Mrs. Tweedie's group and it grew very quickly due to this large influx of Germans. I had no choice now but to re-evaluate my feelings towards them. I slowly began to accept that second- and third-generation Germans were good people. Logically they could not have had anything to do with the Nazis. The really big thing that helped me in this process was to see Mrs. Tweedie relating to these people, and because of my utter devotion to her, as far as I was concerned, if she accepted them, so would I. Mrs. Tweedie placed great emphasis on tolerance, understanding, compassion and forgiveness. I was not willing to be stuck all my life in negative feelings and with this animosity in my heart. The question I had to ask myself was, "Can I ever forgive the Germans?" My initial reaction was, "No, I can't." Our people were murdered because they were born Jewish. How could I forget? It seemed impossible. And to forgive? Maybe now I could achieve this. These were, after all, very nice people. I have to admit that after a while I became very close to many more of them. I was soon even trusting them to look after my house when Lennie and I would go away on holidays.

I am going to relate a number of incidents, including some very deep spiritual realizations I had, that finally enabled me to exorcise my negative feelings towards the Germans.

The first of these happened in one of our meetings when my German tenant told Mrs. Tweedie and our group of a dream she had in which she remembered the words *Savta savati*. Several people at the meeting including one Vedic scholar tried to interpret this but couldn't. They thought it might have been the Sanskrit word *Sarasvati*. This is the name of a well known spiritual poetess and was a name that had been given to me by Swami Vishnudevananda in a beautiful initiation I had received from him in a ceremony in Regents Park in London long before I had met Mrs. Tweedie. She asked us all in the room whether any of us could make any sense of this dream and it occurred to me that the Regents Park initiation was a possible interpretation, but what seemed more likely was that this was Hebrew and not a Sanskrit word. I then asked Mrs. Tweedie if I could say what I thought this dream meant and she said I could. In Hebrew, Savta Savati means "Grandmother, I am satisfied." I was suddenly struck by a very strong, irrational and inexplicable feeling that I had been related to my German tenant in a previous life, and that "grandmother," not in the literal sense, means "ancient connection" or the receiving of an ancient wisdom. I felt that I clearly had an ancient connection with my German tenant. Mrs. Tweedie accepted this interpretation from me and as a result an even greater bond grew between me and my new German friends. I don't believe in coincidence, but synchronicity has meaning for me. Perhaps we had to meet again in this life to work through some things. It certainly helped me to overcome my problems with German people because it reinforced how all human beings and thus all nationalities are connected in spirit and that I had actually been spiritually related to one of these Germans. This realization took all the venom out of my aversion to the Germans and neutralised it. I was slowly realising that my feelings were totally illogical. Mrs. Tweedie observed this happening to me. She had on many occasions asked me if I wanted to accompany her on trips to Germany, but I had always found some feeble excuses not to go; often these excuses were based on my financial situation. I always protested that I could not afford it, conveniently forgetting that on many past trips I had taken with her to other countries, the finances had somehow always worked out. One day she said, "Listen, Miriam, I'm going off to Hart, near Munich, and I would like you to come. Now either you want to progress on this path or you don't, which is it going to be?" This question brought me face-to-face with my phobia about the Germans. I knew that now was the time where I had to reconcile my past if I was to move on and face my future. I knew I would be safe with Mrs. Tweedie wherever she wanted me to go. I trusted her one hundred percent.

So I, Mrs. Tweedie and a large group of her followers set off on a journey to Hart in Germany. She asked me to take some yoga classes there. We all stayed in various guest houses and I stayed with a German family. The landlady there took an instant liking to me; my speaking German was helpful. She often invited me for coffee, tea and meals, and she told me she had never come across such a beautiful group of people as us. She said we were all so loving and peaceful. She asked me if I would take her to some of our meetings and she also came to one of our Sufi parties. I could see we had made a deep impression on her.

Another major incident that I will never forget was when six of us from Mrs. Tweedie's group decided to go for a picnic by a beautiful flowing river in the Hart region. We were all having a wonderful time paddling in the river and constructing shapes and symbols from the stones on the river bank when suddenly we heard a tremendous roaring sound and we looked up to see many skinheads arriving on their bikes. I instantly realised they had spotted the British number plate of our car and meant business. I suddenly felt a shiver run up my spine as I realised these were Nazis that were intending to do us harm. Then I noticed one of the members of our group, a guy named Dan, walking towards them and he started to speak to them. I remember that I could not quite hear the conversation, but I was surprised that Dan could speak German; I had not realised that up to this point. I noticed the situation became very serious and I began to worry for Dan's safety as well as ours. Then suddenly the skinheads got back on their motorcycles and drove off. That was a very close call and I was shaken by the fact that here in Germany I was having a first-hand experience with a fascist group. I had a moment of weakness as all my old feelings about the Germans came rushing back and I asked myself why I had come to Germany. My mind then immediately turned to thoughts of Mrs. Tweedie and her love, tolerance, understanding, compassion and forgiveness. This was another lesson for me.

A very important and redeeming factor that enabled me to forgive the Germans was the many hundreds of requests that I had personally received from them for forgiveness. Many of them came up to me and begged me to forgive their nation for what it had done to the

Jewish people. I started to understand the suffering and guilt of these young Germans. They had never met any Jewish people like me who had actually been through the Holocaust. I gained a lot through these interactions. I knew so much about rejection, pain, suffering and loss myself and could see that many of my new German friends were experiencing something very similar. I remember a particular incident when I was teaching a yoga session in Hart, and we were in a break and I went outside for some fresh air when suddenly I felt some hands resting on my shoulders and I turned around and a girl fell into my arms crying out "Forgive me, forgive me, forgive me." What could I do? I hugged her and I forgave her because it was not her fault. This type of thing happened quite a few times whilst I was in Germany. It also happened to me in Switzerland where there are many German people. I often told these people

Miriam with Irina Tweedie in her garden and the German visitors

to go and visit concentration camps and try to imagine what went on there and see if they can learn from this experience.

One thing that I would like to mention is that many Jews, especially the first generation survivors of the holocaust, are still stuck in a bitter hatred for Germany and Germans. I would certainly still be stuck there if it had not been for Mrs. Tweedie. I am also mindful of the fact that a Nazi Party organizer named George had saved our lives by risking his own through pretending that my sister had typhus, and this enabled us to escape transportation to a death camp.

I decided that I would go with a group of my German friends to Dachau. I had wanted to go to Dachau anyway. I had already been to Ebensee, near Mauthausen where my father and brother were taken. The horrible place in Ebensee where they were forced to work in a quarry was now a children's playground. I found a rock there where I scribbled an inscription of the dates of birth and death of my father and brother.

Going to Dachau was a different experience, and this was also a great help to me in my own reconciliation and forgiveness. I went with a small group of Germans. I have to admit that my feelings that day were very complex; part of me was wanting to rub their noses in it and show them how low and disgusting their people had sunk. On the other hand these were all such nice people and they wanted to go. I must have been difficult to be with on that day. This may sound silly, but I had an enormous bee in my bonnet about being charged for parking at Dachau. Luckily for everybody around me that it was free parking. I was ready to explode if they charged. How on earth would they dare charge us for parking at a crematorium where so many of my people were murdered?

After we had parked, I gathered everyone together and told them that I wanted them all to scream as we walk into this concentration camp. I said, "Listen, everyone, I want you to scream and shout until your guts come out; you will do this because those people who were slaughtered here had nobody who would listen to them, so we are going to do their screaming on their behalf. They had no chance to scream, so we will scream for them, and THEN, when it's all over, we will sit down and meditate."

This exercise was extremely moving for us all. As we all screamed, we started to feel the pain of the thousands who had died on this spot. This perhaps was the most important thing I did to help my own reconciliation

Miriam and Irina Tweedie with a group of friends and German students

process. I needed to cry for all those who had perished under the boots of the Nazi conquerors, slaughtered in the most horrible ways, and the fact that I had cried with the descendants of the slaughterers themselves had enormous significance for all of us. It felt like we had all undergone a cleansing process.

What Mrs. Tweedie did for me will always remain somewhat of a mystery. I accepted the teaching I received from her and it was ingrained in my heart. Much of what Mrs. Tweedie gave me was given during the night, when one is not consciously aware, so I know that much of what I received was on an unconscious level. Mrs. Tweedie said that she was often accused of being a witch. On one level she found this accusation very amusing, but on a more serious note she knew that she was touching people's hearts and infusing them with knowledge in a mystical way through the unconscious mind. She called me an "intuitive mystic," maybe because I was open to receive the inner knowledge.

My philosophy of life is to live and let live—let others live according to their own light. We came into this life with two attributes—to serve and to worship. My goal in life is to help people, to raise consciousness, and to live in the present. Love endows us with hope and courage. Love gives us insight and inspiration. Love takes us home to the Source of life. Love is everything. Love conquers all.

The journey still goes on…

Miriam, Martin, Allison and Lennie

Miriam and Martin

"See that bird in the sky. It leaves no traces.
That is how we must be.
To follow the spiritual path we give a blank cheque,
not knowing if we will get anything in return."

Irina Tweedie

CHAPTER ELEVEN

Aphorisms and Sayings of Mrs. Tweedie

Mrs. Tweedie, during her group meetings, used aphorisms or quotations which were significant to various situations or relevant to one person or to the group. The following is a collection of these sayings that were recorded from memory by Pat Brock from these group meetings, and she kindly gave her permission for me to use them here.

To me, these sayings are so special and significant that I wanted to include them here and share with the reader. I am often referring to them, especially when I'm with friends or students. My hope is that the reader will receive what they need through these sayings and will help them on their life's journey in the way it has helped me.

∞

Sufi guidance given by Mrs. Tweedie
during group meetings held in her home
over a period of some years

January, 1980

The Will of the Atma, the divine essence within.
Not to be confused with the desire of the personality or little ego Or of the mind, which loathes to be ignored.
When it is confused, it appears to attract unpleasant situations and adverse conditions—the enemy.

Sometimes these are like tests, as with the biblical story of Job, a testing of the two wills.

When one bows down and accepts things as they are, the way becomes clear and miracles take place.

It does not mean that one should be submissive. There are times when one must stand up, be firm, and take positive action. The problem is knowing which and when is the right way.

It is a question of balance, discernment, and discrimination.

Take the bull by the horns, but let the lamb lead you through darkness.

April 1980

The disciple is like a pendulum. The peace and bliss of the beloved comes and goes, thus creating the longing, the cause for the effect.

This is the effort.

~

Where one is depressed, one should not say that it will pass. Deep down one knows that it will. One should accept it. Say to oneself, "I accept this depression."

~

Do not become attached to anything, not even spiritual practices.

~

1980

We do not protect ourselves from others. No barriers. Protection from evil forces is to love. We are so full of love they cannot stand it.

~

What does it matter if someone drains us? A few deep breaths, tuning into That, and we are recovered. And someone else has benefited from our company.

~

A truly spiritual experience cannot be understood by the mind.

~

Dreams are sometimes to work out karma of the mind.

~

Cancer? One does not interfere with cancer. It is a way of getting rid of physical karma.

~

When one is in pain, offer it to the Beloved.

~

We do not wear special clothes. It creates a barrier between us and other people.

~

Reading? Why, to gain more knowledge, to know more than I do? Reading, knowledge, is unnecessary.

~

To experience oneself, that is true knowledge. Curiosity. It's pedestrian.

~

Watch out for the casual remark. It may be for you.

~

Sufis must earn their living.

One must not allow states of consciousness to interfere with everyday work and life.

The mystic must keep his feet on the ground and hold up the vault of the sky with his head.

~

We, we are branded by God, like the animals are branded. We come into this world branded. We cannot escape.

When Jesus talked about his sheep, it has deep meaning. "If we ascend into Heaven, Thou art there. If I make my bed in Hell, Thou art there also."

We cannot escape.

~

Guruji said:
"We are people of peace, we do not divide. We unite."
Guruji's life was devoted to the single objective of uniting hearts. All of us who continue his work, we do the same.
Sounds easy, but it is the most difficult thing in the world to unite hearts.

~

February 1986

Our path is between Bhakti (devotion and surrender) and Karma (action).

~

The soul always agrees to death. Somewhere the soul has said "yes" to death.

~

Guruji said:

"Like the factory. The general manager says one must go, and instructs the personnel manager. He puts it off, delays it, but eventually has to do as the general manager says."

~

Our life is given to those we guide. We have no friends. Sometimes it can be very lonely.

~

We should not be attached to spiritual life. We should not be attached to meditation.

~

Men and women. They need each other. We were not meant to live alone.

~

May 1986

A mystical experience. Don't try to describe it. You will destroy it.

~

The problems begin. It is difficult to reconcile the experience with the world around us. But it is all one and the same.

~

On our path, Kundalini is awakened gently. When a human being is awakened, he is a human being plus. That "plus" is incognito. Who can say what it is.

~

July 16, 1986

Meditation. The objective is to still the mind. This is very difficult for many people. The mind has a will of its own and doesn't want to be put to rest.

Imagine a space within you where God's love dwells. Put yourself, all of you, the physical as well as the mind, in that space, wherein you are surrounded by love.

~

Thoughts will still come. Observe them and let them pass through. After a while they will become less frequent and eventually they will disappear. It takes many years. For some it is more difficult than for others.

~

One day there will be a blissful state of peace.

~

For those who have practised this meditation for a long time and reached this state, it is not necessary to use the imagination.

~

July 21, 1986

This meditation awakens a certain kind of energy (Kundalini) seated at the base of the spine.

In the beginning it can affect the waterworks, and in some cases arouse the sexual energy. It is the same energy. As it moves up it can affect other organs in the body—the digestive system, the heartbeat (the heart chakra).

Everyone is different. It is not the same for everyone. Some people come into this life already having reached a certain stage on the spiritual path. For them the effects may begin with the heartbeat.

~

July 28, 1986

There is a hidden place within your heart where God is, the Beloved. We Sufis call God the Beloved.

Find that place.

Imagine all of yourself in that place, that space of love. Do not leave anything outside, not even a small fingernail.

The thoughts will come—what you did yesterday, what you must do today. Drown these thoughts in the love within that space.

Love is a more dynamic force than the mind. The feeling quality is more dynamic than thinking.

It takes years but one day you will be able to still the mind instantly.

~

August 18, 1986

Never, never is money involved in real spiritual guidance.

~

If we are given insight into the Reality behind the "appearance," it is a gift, a grace. And as such, it is passed on.

~

The spiritual "teachers" are elder brothers or sisters and, as one guides one's younger brothers, sisters, friends, in the affairs of everyday life, so it is on the spiritual path.

~

One is never expected to do more than one is capable of.

~

1986

I am not a teacher.
I am not a guide.
I let people in, and, if necessary, I kick them out.
I do nothing. I merely create the atmosphere here.
Everything else is done for me.

~

March 16, 1987

We look for perfection. It isn't possible. We are just poor sinners doing our best. There has to be a compromise.

Once we have glimpsed That which is perfect, we look for perfection in everything and try to perfect that which we do. No! Life is a compromise.

We must learn to compromise.

~

April 3, 1987

Listening to the inner voice. That is what we are doing here. Learning to recognize and listen to the inner voice.

~

It helps to have a guru. But guru is not one hundred percent necessary.

When we know the inner voice, that becomes your guru.

The attitude changes, outwardly we remain the same person.

~

August 13, 1987

How did I come to meet Guruji?

I read a book on Buddhism and lost God. I thought I was going mad and kept talking to people about it. Of course they were not interested.

The thought of going into a big void with no God to cling to...

~

September 23, 1987

The aura reverses its direction, going inward. To a clairvoyant it looks as though the person is dying.

~

During the meditation, initially the outer mind continues to be active.

Later, after practice, the inner mind comes to the fore.

Then both the inner and outer become part of the universal mind.

~

Esoteric knowledge was previously given only to those in the group. Now it is to be made known generally.

~

November 9, 1987

I want to explain to you the effects of deep meditation. Sometimes it is necessary to repeat myself.

~

The aura, the magnetic field surrounding the body, works in reverse.

Energy manifests itself through matter, which enables us earthly beings to live and carry on our various activities.

~

In deep meditation the reverse is the case. It is a little like dying but not, of course, dying in the sense generally understood. The heart continues to beat and breathing goes on, even though it becomes shallow.

The mind and body cease to use energy and it—the mind—is temporarily suspended.

The mind and body are different entities. Each small cell of the body has its own independent life cycle.

~

November 11, 1987

We try to keep the ancient tradition. Guruji changed some things because of my psychology, but not much, and we keep the tradition here.

We have no rules, no disciplines. For many this is not accepted. They want rules. For the Germans this is especially difficult. They like to be organised, regimented. One asked a companion, speaking of me…

"What does she do?"

"Nothing."

"But what do you do?"

"Whatever you like."

You see, it is not easy. We shall never be many. Guruji used to say.

November 11, 1987

This path is only for the few. No, there are no disciplines and we are free.

We must discipline ourselves. And we are alone. We learn to stand alone.

Many people come here. Some have been with me for a long time, a nucleus.

Many come for one or two years, and then they go elsewhere.

It is not for everybody.

~

November 16, 1987

One must be one-pointed, like the arrow, say the Sufis. Single-minded. If one wants the whole Truth.

Some people who come here, they get a little bit of Truth. They are not prepared to give up everything.

One lady, who writes poetry, said she wanted the whole truth! I asked her about the poetry and she said she couldn't give that up. It came to her through a guide and people enjoyed it.

So I said, why not be satisfied with that?

Yes, one must give up everything. That does not mean giving away everything. I had to. It is not being attached to anything one has.

And one must have good health. This meditation weakens the body.

~

November 17, 1987

I was a librarian. One thinks of librarianship as being interesting work. But much of it was entering records. Once I counted. For each book I had to make nine entries.

After a while all jobs became boring, no matter what. Yet it is a discipline. One should look upon it as a discipline.

~

November 18, 1987

On the spiritual path one has to forget everything else. This like a love affair. When you love someone, you think of no one else. This is the great love affair, for God, That, the Beloved. Whatever you like to call him—It.

And one has to forgive. If anyone is here who is not prepared for this, then let them leave.

Guruji used to say: "One must not be distracted by non-essentials." Those who are not prepared, let them leave, or I personally will throw them out.

Those of you who have been here for some time, they know. I have done it. Sometimes bodily. I push them out the door.

I speak my mind. I am not like the English. They do things more subtly, gently. I'm not like that. I'm not here to help you with your problems. I create them. Problems for you to overcome.

~

December, 1987

The great ones can do no evil. What is evil? It is ignorance.

We can do evil. They cannot. They are so quickened they are unable to do it.

One has to rise above temptations, and then there is no temptation.

~

August 2, 1987

The yogi is content because he accepts everything. If one accepts, then it is easy.

~

The eyes are not good. This one, it may go blind. Will it go blind before I die, or will I die before it is blind? What does it matter? I am old.

~

Every day we surrender to something. To the bus which drives us, to the omelette we are making, to the child who needs our attention.

I don't see these people sitting in front of me. Why do you think that is? I will tell you.

They are part of me, so I don't see them.

~

August 11, 1988

What is given to us is not for ourselves, but to pass on to others.

If someone asks your advice, or questions you, then you answer as best you can. This person becomes your responsibility.

~

We are not gurus. We are just ordinary people on the Path. Someone ahead is trying to help us and it is our responsibility to help others. Spiritual path is like a ladder. Anyone of us can have a meditation group.

~

If you do not reach realization, Guruji will be there to take you with him at the moment of death.

~

You will make mistakes as we all do at times. I have made mistakes. Then you tell that person about it.

It is good to make mistakes sometimes. The humiliation of admitting a mistake is good for us.

~

October 20, 1988

The appearance behind the action is what is important.

There are great beings all over the world in important positions, in governments, in politics. Wherever there is trouble in the world, you will find one of our line, trying to pull strings.

We are beyond the law of man, yet we must obey the law of the land. And we must set an example.

~

If I am given things, I can keep them or refuse them, or give them away. But I must not ask unless I need something. This is the tradition.
Oh yes, for others we can ask.

~

October 20, 1988

And if I receive orders—orders are given by the higher beings who guide our lives—they must be followed exactly.

~

I cannot change anything. And if my little ego says, "Oh, but this is the West and this way will work better" or "for this person this way will not work," it is ineffective.
This is the tradition.

~

October 24, 1988

See that bird in the sky.
It leaves no traces.
That is how we must be.
To follow the spiritual path you must give a blank cheque, not knowing whether you will get anything in return.

~

December 11, 1989

Guidance? For some it is a voice. Not the voice a schizophrenic hears. No, it is a voice giving direction when needed.

For others, a strong prompting to do or not to do something.

And it can be a small thought entering the consciousness quietly, which has nothing to do with one's surroundings or what one is doing.

Discrimination is important. One must be able to discriminate.

~

What is being done?

We are cooking new persons. And while the cooking process is taking place, oh, how it hurts.

They are cooked in soup.

~

February 19, 1990

It is not possible to be constantly aware of loving a person.

Sometimes one feels love, then another time one may be indifferent.

You may even think that love for one's husband or wife has ceased to exist. Then just wait until that person doesn't get home on time and you begin to worry. Then the love is there. I was married twice, and had other relationships of course, when I was young.

But, and I have tested this, one can be constantly in love with the Beloved.

I am rather sceptical. I must test things, several times, until I know I'm sure.

The meditation is the most important. When you do this meditation, love enters your heart.

~

March 19, 1990

The body has to become refined to receive a higher energy. The nervous system is affected. There will be problems.

~

Each one of us in this group who attends the meditations, whether regularly or when they can, has a contribution to make.

~

Once the connection has been made, and the commitment, it isn't necessary to be here all the time. Work is done in the night.

There are those who can only visit here once a year, or less. This doesn't matter. The connection is there.

~

March 26, 1996

I have no disciples. I will not be put on a pedestal. I just am.

~

Inner workings, they take place. You do it yourselves.

~

Dreams are important. They tell the person something.

We tell dreams here. That person gets attention and others learn to interpret.

~

When people try to put me on a pedestal, I behave badly. You know. I can behave very badly. I can swear too, in English as well as Russian.

~

No, I have no disciples. This is my home. I have here who I wish.

You are my guests.

~

March 19, 1990

No, I do not believe in the healing qualities of crystals. Crystals are crystals. Any stone or metal can be magnetized; copper especially.

A person, yes. It is the person who has the healing qualities. A powerful person.

~

May 19, 1990

I want to talk to you again about the mantra: **Allah** *Al* with the outward breath, *Lah* with the inward breath.
Al is the equivalent of the definite article. *Lah* means nothing. No thing.
When we breathe in, we take in *prakriti,* cosmic energy.
With the pause between inward and outward breath, the soul experiences bliss, a split second of being in touch with God, or the Beloved. So short a time it is not noticeable.
I say "God" so that everyone knows what I mean, but to give the Absolute a name is to limit it.

~

May 21, 1990

Lah, which is NOTHING shows the soul we are aware, we co-operate with it.
Being aware is important. It's what spiritual life is about.
Spiritual life is simple, but it is not easy.
We live in the present.
When I walk, I am walking. When I make an omelette, the omelette has my attention.
It is surrender. Surrender to that which we are doing in the present.

~

There is another reason for the **Allah** mantra.

Our minds are always busy. We think of this and that. We have conversations with ourselves, with other people.

The mantra helps to quieten the mind.

Do the mantra all day.

Eventually the mantra takes over. It enters the bloodstream and becomes automatic, in the unconscious.

~

October 29, 1990

There is no love here without conflict.

~

November 19, 1990

Beware of the sense of security. There is no security. Spiritual life is like walking on water.

There is no perfection, for nobody, on this earth.

1990

When we pray for others, we think of the person. We ask for peace for him. We visualise the person as being well and peaceful. But then we surrender to "Thy Will be done."

We do not ask for anything else, not for the person to live, or to die. Only for peace, and then leave it in God's hands, and let the thought go to where it belongs.

Do not hold the thought. It does no good to hold the thought.

We Sufis, we surrender always to the will of God.

Prayer is prayer. We ask for nothing.

We pray, and then surrender to prayer to God's Will.

~

If you love someone, let them be free. If they come back, they are yours. If not, they never were.

~

Glossary of Indian Terms

Chakras In Hindu and tantric/yogic traditions and other belief systems *chakras* are energy points or knots in the subtle body. They are located at the physical counterparts of the major plexuses of arteries, veins and nerves. *Chakras* are part of the subtle body, not the physical body, and as such are the meeting points of the subtle (non-physical) energy channels, called *nadi*. *Nadis* are channels in the subtle body through which the life force *(prana)* or vital energy moves. Various scriptural texts and teachings present a different number of *chakras*. There are many *chakras* in the subtle human body according to the tantric texts, but there are seven *chakras* that are considered to be the most important ones.

Their name derives from the Sanskrit word for "wheel" or "turning," but in the yogic context a better translation of the word is "vortex" or "whirlpool."

Dhyāna means meditation in Hinduism, Buddhism and Jainism. It refers to various states of *samadhi*, a state of consciousness in which the observer detaches from several qualities of the mind. In this state one has become firm and stable and everything that is appearing is noticed but not identified to. *Dhyana* is the awareness of the observer (witness) yet inclusive of mind, body, senses and surroundings, however not identified with it, deepening of which leads to *samadhi*. The *Sutta Pitaka* describes four levels of *dhyana*, called *jhana*, each of increasing depth.

The Zen tradition has been named after this meditative state, though in Chinese Buddhism *dhyana* may refer to all kinds of meditation techniques and their preparatory practices which can be used to attain *samadhi*.

Hatha Yoga Hatha means sun and the moon. Yoga means union of higher self with lower self. In the West it is interpreted as a physical yoga.

Ida *see Nadi*

Kundalini (Sanskrit kuṇḍalinī,) stems from yogic philosophy as a form of feminine *shakti* or "corporeal energy." Kundalini is described within Eastern religious, or spiritual, tradition as an indwelling spiritual energy that can be awakened in order to purify the subtle system and ultimately to bestow the state of Yoga, or Divine Union, upon the "seeker" of truth. The Yoga Upanishads describe Kundalini as lying "coiled" at the base of the spine, represented as either a goddess or sleeping serpent waiting to be awakened. In modern commentaries, Kundalini has been called an unconscious, instinctive, or libidinal force.

It is reported that Kundalini awakening results in deep meditation, enlightenment and bliss. This awakening involves the Kundalini physically moving up the central channel to reside within the Sahasrara Chakra above the head. This movement of Kundalini is felt by the presence of a cool or, in the case of imbalance, a warm breeze across the palms of the hands or the soles of the feet. Many systems of yoga focus on the awakening of Kundalini through meditation, pranayama breathing, the practice of asana and chanting of mantras. In physical terms, one commonly reported Kundalini experience is a feeling like electric current running along the spine.

Nāḍi (tube, "pipe") are the channels through which, in traditional Indian medicine and spiritual science, the energies of the subtle body are said to flow. They connect at special points of intensity called "*chakras.*"

In normal biological reference, a *nadi* can be translated into "nerve" in English. However, in yogic, and specifically in Kundalini yoga reference, a *nadi* can be thought of as a channel (not an anatomical structure). In regard to Kundalini yoga, there are three of these *nadis*: *Ida*, *pingala*, and *sushumna*. *Ida* lies to the left of the spine, whereas *pingala* is to the right side of the spine, mirroring the *ida*. *Sushumna* runs along the spinal cord in the center, through the seven *chakras*—*Mooladhaar* at the base, and *Sahasrar* at the top (or crown) of the head. It is at the base of this *sushumna* where the *Kundalini* lies coiled in three and a half coils, in a dormant or sleeping state.

Pingala *see Nadi*

Samadhi in Hinduism, Buddhism, Jainism, Sikhism and yogic schools is a higher level of concentrated meditation, or *dhyāna*. In the yoga tradition, it is the eighth and final limb identified in the *Yoga Sūtras* of Patañjali.

It has been described as a non-dualistic state of consciousness in which the consciousness of the experiencing subject becomes one with the experienced object, and in which the mind becomes still, one-pointed, or concentrated while the person remains conscious. In Buddhism, it can also refer to an abiding in which mind becomes very still but does not merge with the object of attention, and is thus able to observe and gain insight into the changing flow of experience.

Shushumna *see Nadi*

Tyaga This term refers to The Path of *Tyaga*, the path of complete renunciation. According to Bhai Sahib, "... there are two roads: the Road of *Dhyana*, the slow one, and the Road of *Tyaga*, of complete Renunciation, of Surrender: this is the Direct Road, the Path of Fire, the Path of Love." (*Daughter of Fire*, p. 237. Golden Sufi Center)

Yoga nidra or "yogi sleep" is a sleep-like state which yogis report to experience during their meditations. Yoga nidra, lucid sleeping, is among the deepest possible states of relaxation while still maintaining full consciousness.

About the Author

MIRIAM FREEDMAN was born in Czechoslovakia. Many of her close family were murdered in the holocaust, and by sheer luck Miriam managed to escape the same fate by hiding with her mother, sister, and other family members. After the war she emigrated to Israel where she studied in Jerusalem and qualified as a primary school teacher and then taught for seventeen years in Israel and England in both state and private schools.

In 1967 she met Swami Visnudevananda in London who initiated her yoga training. She later studied the Iyengar method and in 1976 took her diploma with the British Wheel of Yoga. Miriam became a greatly respected yoga teacher. In the early 1980s she increased her knowledge of alternative therapies through auto-genic training, reflexology, massage and counseling. In 1979 her whole life changed when she came across a meditation group run by a Russian lady named Irina Tweedie. Mrs. Tweedie was a very powerful and mystical teacher who propagated the teachings of a non-denominational Sufi line that stretches back into the mist of time. Miriam opens up her personal dream world, which is not unlike Carl Gustav Jung's, to reveal layers of centuries-old mystical teachings that inform of inner realities that are there for us all to explore.

Praise for *Love Is Always the Answer*

"It is unusual to be taken by the hand through someone's intimate spiritual unfoldment in such a disarming and compelling way.

"The trajectory of Miriam's life—from its dark beginnings under the terrors of Nazi Europe, to the attainment of her heart's light and spirit's power in London under her spiritual teacher—demonstrates the true organic nature of the spiritual path.

"That longing in the heart which set Miriam on her journey is something many will recognize in themselves; the courage she displays in her commitment to the search for spiritual knowledge was no less required there than it was under the Nazis; and the intense experiences she underwent in her inner world and dream life are not only a privilege to read, but show yet again how true are the words of C.G. Jung when he stated that to undertake the ultimate inner journey requires the whole strength of the hero within you.

"The alchemist's prize—the Philosopher's Stone— is no less than the enlightened heart which Miriam has attained to, and the beautiful light and power of that heart is what shines through and infuses this most moving story. Love, indeed, is the beginning and the end of it, though there is no end..."

—Séza Magdalena Eccles,
magazine and book publisher

"Your remarkable autobiography is truly a life-affirming story of courage and resilience in the face of the tragedy of the Holocaust."

—Daniel Taub, Ambassador of Israel to the Court of St. James's

"An autobiography of a Holocaust survivor who has found her own remarkable way to live with the trauma from her past. An inspiring and positive story of how an individual found alternative ways to deal with her emotions and the past. We can all learn something from this book."

—Aviva Trup, RGN, RMN, BSc Community Health, Service Manager, Holocaust Survivor Centre

"I have shared many moments along the road with Miriam to discover the True nature of our Soul. *Love Is Always the Answer* is a testimony of how one person can go beyond even the most challenging of circumstances to realise the gift that God planted deep within our hearts. It is the ever-burning Divine Spark of Love which can never go out! No tragedy, no person, no belief can take it away and this book takes you on that journey.

—Ginger Gilmour, artist and writer

"This is a book that everyone should read. There are no 'extra-ordinary' people ... just ordinary people who deal with extra-ordinary events, and Miriam Freedman as a child had to deal with the extra-ordinary events which unfortunately have shaped the 20th century.

"Miriam's story is a graphic and horrific account of what happened to her as a Jewish child in Nazi Germany. It is a testament to the strength and courage of one human being caught up in the madness of war. We never know what our fate will be and how we might deal with extreme suffering. What we can know, though, is that as human beings we can find strength in adversity. Miriam is one of the strongest people I know. Despite her horrific history she has the biggest heart and is one of the most loving people I have ever met.

"You will read this book and never again will you look at a human being and presume you know them."

—Judith Ashton, psychotherapist/body therapist, former student of Irina Tweedie